Agricultural Risk and Insurance in India

Agricultural Risk and Insurance in India

Problems and Prospects

S.S. Raju
Ramesh Chand

ACADEMIC FOUNDATION
NEW DELHI

First published in 2009
by

ACADEMIC FOUNDATION
4772-73 / 23 Bharat Ram Road, (23 Ansari Road),
Darya Ganj, New Delhi - 110 002 (India).
Phones : 23245001 / 02 / 03 / 04.
Fax : +91-11-23245005.
E-mail : books@academicfoundation.com
www. academicfoundation.com

Cataloging in Publication Data--DK
Courtesy: D.K. Agencies (P) Ltd. <docinfo@dkagencies.com>

Raju, S. S.
Agricultural risk and insurance in India : problems and prospects / S.S. Raju and Ramesh Chand.
p. cm.
With special reference to Andhra Pradesh, India.
Includes bibliographical references (p.).
Includes index.
ISBN 13: 9788171887651
ISBN 10: 8171887651

1. Farm risks--India. 2. Farm risks--India--Andhra Pradesh. 3. Crop insurance--India. 4. Crop insurance--India--Andhra Pradesh. 5. Agricultural insurance--India. 6. Agriculture--Economic aspects--India. I. Ramesh Chand, 1956-, joint author. II. Title.

DDC 368.12100954 22

Typeset by Italics India, New Delhi.
Printed and bound in India.

CONTENTS

List of Tables

Tables

Preface

The need to protect farmers against high fluctuations in yields and prices in agriculture has been a continuing concern of agricultural policy. In India, agricultural insurance is one of the instruments for protecting farmers from wide agricultural variability. Nearly a century ago J.S. Chakravarthy introduced the idea of rainfall insurance based on area approach for the Mysore State and for India as a whole with a view to insuring farmers against drought. However, the coverage under various agricultural insurance schemes launched in the country has been very low in the past. This study aims at identifying the problems and prospects of agricultural insurance in India, and suggest ways and means to expand the coverage and improve effectiveness of agricultural insurance programmes in the country.

The book is based on the work done at National Centre for Agricultural Economics and Policy Research (NCAP) of ICAR, New Delhi. We express our thanks to the Centre for providing resources for undertaking this work. We express our gratitude to Dr. P.K. Joshi, Director, NCAP for the encouragement and valuable suggestion he made from time to time in improving the quality and scope of the work. We are grateful to Mr. K.N. Rao, Manager, Agricultural Insurance Company of India Ltd. (AIC), New Delhi, for his constant support in primary data collection and helpful suggestions in the course of the study.

We also thank the farmers and officials of the AIC, agricultural department, bankers, academicians and other representatives in New Delhi as well as Andhra Pradesh for sharing valuable data about agricultural insurance. Finally, we would like to place on record the help rendered by Ms. Umeeta Ahuja and Mr. Deepak Tanwar in preparing the computer script.

The book provides estimates of risk involved in farm production, prices and farm income which in turn underline the need to go for insurance of agriculture. It provides a critique of agricultural insurance schemes implemented from time to time and presents an overview of prevailing public and private sector involvement in agriculture insurance. The book discusses limitations of the existing insurance schemes and proposes changes in design of schemes and public policy to take insurance to the needy farmers.

The views and opinions expressed in this book are entirely those of the authors, and do not in any manner reflect the views or opinion of the organisation to which they belong.

S.S. Raju
Ramesh Chand

Abbreviations

AGROSEGURO	:	Agrupacion Espanola de Entidades Ase guradoras de los Seguros Agrarious Co mbinados
AI	:	Actual Income
AIC	:	Agricultural Insurance Company of India
APC	:	Agricultural Price Commission
APMC	:	Agricultural Produce Market Committee
AY	:	Actual Yield
CBs	:	Commercial Banks
CCEs	:	Crop Cutting Experiments
CCIS	:	Comprehensive Crop Insurance Scheme
CCS	:	Consorcio de Compensacion de Seguros
ECIS	:	Experimental Crop Insurance Scheme
ENESA	:	Entidas Estatal de Seguros Agrariors
FCIC	:	Federal Crop Insurance Corporation
FHP	:	Farm Harvest Prices
FIIS	:	Farm Income Insurance Scheme
FIs	:	Financial Institutions
GCES	:	General Crop Estimation Survey
GI	:	Guaranteed Income
GIC	:	General Insurance Corporation
GM	:	Genetically Modified
GoI	:	Government of India
GP	:	*Gram Panchayat*

GR	:	Gross Returns
GY	:	Guaranteed yield
ICAR	:	Indian Council of Agricultural Research
ICICI	:	Industrial Credit Investment Corporation of India
IL	:	Indemnity Limit
IMD	:	Indian Meteorological Department
IRDA	:	Insurance Regulatory Development Authority
IRDP	:	Integrated Rural Development Programme
ITGI	:	IFFCO-Tokio General Insurance
MOFA	:	Ministry of Food and Agriculture
MSP	:	Minimum Support Price
NAIS	:	National Agricultural Insurance Scheme
NAP	:	National Agricultural Policy
NCIS	:	National Crop Insurance Service
NGO	:	Non-Governmental Organisation
PCIC	:	Philippines Crop Insurance Corporation
PCIS	:	Pilot Crop Insurance Scheme
PPP	:	Public Private Partnership
RI	:	Rainfall Insurance
RMA	:	Risk Management Agency
RRBs	:	Regional Rural Bank
SD	:	Standard Deviation
SI	:	Sum Insured
SIG	:	Social Initiative Group
USA	:	United States of America
USDA	:	United States Department of Agriculture
WBCIS	:	Weather Based Crop Insurance Scheme
WTO	:	World Trade Organization

1

Introduction

Agriculture production and farm incomes in India are frequently affected by natural disasters such as droughts, floods, cyclones, storms, landslides, and earthquakes. Vulnerability of agriculture production to these disasters is compounded by the outbreak of epidemics and man-made disasters such as fire, sale of spurious seeds, fertilisers and pesticides, and price crashes, etc. All these events severely affect farmers through loss in production and farm income, and they are beyond the control of the farmers. With the growing commercialisation of agriculture, the magnitude of loss due to unfavourable eventualities is increasing. The question is how to protect farmers by minimising such losses. Agricultural insurance is considered an important mechanism to effectively address the risk to output and income resulting from various natural and man-made events. Agricultural insurance is a means of protecting the agriculturist against financial losses to agriculture sector due to uncertainties arising from named or unforeseen perils beyond their control (AIC, 2008). Unfortunately, agricultural insurance in the country has not made much headway even though the need to protect Indian farmers from agriculture variability has been a continuing concern of India's agriculture policy. According to the National Agriculture Policy 2000, "despite technological and economic advancements, the condition of farmers continues to be unstable due to natural calamities and price fluctuations." In some extreme cases, these unfavourable events become one of the factors leading to farmers' suicides which are now assuming serious proportions (Raju and Chand, 2007). The conventional insurance covers only production risk while market risk is assuming high importance. For a section of farming community, the minimum support prices (MSP) for certain crops provide some income stability but for most of the crops and in most of the states, MSP is only notional (Chand, 2003). During recent years, mechanisms like contract farming have been established which are expected to provide some insurance against price fluctuations directly or indirectly.

Various methods have been adopted by the government for helping farming community to compensate, at least partially, for loss of their crops through natural calamities. Reduction or suspension of land rent taxes, moratorium, input subsidies, scaling down or waiving of accumulated agricultural debts (example, Debt Waiver and Debt Relief Scheme, 2008), and direct relief from the Calamity Relief Fund of the Union government are the more usual of the methods applied so far. Useful though these means have been to the farmers in the past and are likely to be in the future, their great deficiency is that farmers cannot expect them as a right, but rather only as a concession. Secondly, the continued prospects of relief are liable to 'soften' its receipts and are also likely to be questioned by the non-farming community.

In a country where agriculture is at the mercy of the vagaries of the monsoon and other factors beyond the control of the farmer, the importance of agricultural insurance is not in doubt and needs no emphasis (Dandekar, 1976). Insurance provides people with a reasonable degree of security and assurance that they will be protected in the event of a calamity or failure of any sort. The modern insurance sector can play a major role here, and considerably strengthen the financial security of farmers. Agricultural insurance is a more efficient instrument and an effective institutionalised mechanism for dealing with the problem. It helps to streamline the relief efforts, and reduces the direct and indirect costs on the national economy.

Agriculture insurance in the broad sense includes insurance of crops, livestock, fisheries, forestry, sericulture, etc. Realising the importance of agriculture insurance in the country, the Union Finance Minister in his general budget speech for 2002-03 announced the Agriculture Insurance Company (AIC) of India Limited as an exclusive organisation for agriculture insurance. The newly formed AIC took over crop insurance activities from the General Insurance Corporation

(GIC) of India in April 2003. The AIC is promoted by the GIC, which holds 35 per cent, NABARD which holds 30 per cent, and four public sector general insurance companies, which hold 8.75 per cent each. The AIC has an authorised share capital of Rs.1500 crores, an initial capital of Rs.200 crores. In the current scenario, the AIC is the largest body offering insurance cover to cultivators in India.

1.1 Farmers' Strategies for Risk Mitigation

The risk bearing capacity of an average farmer is very limited, particularly in rain dependent semi-arid tropics. Further, a large farm household or a wealthy farmer is able to spread risk over time and space in several ways; he can use stored grains or savings during bad years, he can diversify his crop production across different plots. At a higher level of income and staying power, the farmer would opt for higher average yields or profits over a period of time even if it is achieved at the cost of high annual variability on output (Rao *et al.*, 1988). The situation of small and resource poor farmers is totally different. In the absence of formal risk sharing mechanisms, farmers rely on traditional modes and methods to deal with production risk in agriculture. Many cropping strategies and farming practices have been adopted in the absence of crop insurance for stabilising crop revenue. Availability and effectiveness of these risk management strategies or insurance surrogates depend on public policies (Walker and Jodha, 1986). Nevertheless, farmers' own mechanisms for loss management or risk diffusion are found to be very expensive based on a study on risk averting tendencies of the farmers and available strategies for shifting risk in arid and semi-arid regions (Binswanger, 1980). It is further argued that farmers' own measures to reduce the risk in farming in semi-arid tropical India were not only costly but also relatively ineffective in reducing risk in farming and to adjust to drought and scarcity conditions (Jodha, 1981).

1.2 Agriculture Insurance for Risk Mitigation

Agricultural insurance is one method by which farmers can stabilise farm income and investment, and guard against disastrous effect of losses due to natural hazards. Agricultural insurance can also be designed to protect against risk of price crash or market risk. Besides income stabilisation, crop insurance also helps the farmers to initiate production activity after a bad agricultural year. It cushions the shock of crop losses by providing farmers with some amount of protection. It spreads the crop losses over space and time, and helps farmers make more investments in agriculture. It forms an important component of safety-net programmes as is being experienced in many developed countries like the USA and Canada as well as in the European Union. However, one needs to keep in mind that crop insurance should be part of overall risk management strategy. Insurance comes towards the end of risk management process. Insurance is redistribution of the cost of losses of few among many, and cannot prevent economic loss.

There are two major categories of agricultural insurance: single and multi-peril coverage. Single peril coverage offers protection from single hazard while multiple-peril provides protection from several hazards. In India, multi-peril crop insurance programme is being implemented, considering the overwhelming impact of nature on agricultural output and its disastrous consequences on the society, in general, and farmers, in particular. Many of the risks insured under public insurance programme are essentially un-insurable risks. Moreover, they occur frequently and hence are expensive to insure. The financial performance of most of the public crop insurance has been ruinous in both developed and developing countries. The multi-peril crop insurance thus is very expensive, and has to be heavily subsidised (Hazell, 1992).

1.3 Impact of Insurance

As per UNCTAD document (1994), agricultural insurance has many advantages. First, as the agricultural sector is not well organised on institutional lines, it can help agriculture to develop through institutionalised channels and assist in speeding up the process of commercialisation of the sector. Second, it can play a distinct role in securing credit from institutional sources as it provides security to the lending institutions. Third, it provides strength to farmers for a better deal in respect of interest rates in a liberalised interest rate regime.

Four, it can ensure better recovery of loans as the credit agency would receive the payment from the insurance company in the event of production risk. As it has relevance for improving agricultural technology as with the security of insurance, farmers might be more willing to experiment with new technology. Six, crop insurance is an efficient instrument and an institutionalised mechanism for dealing with problems of natural calamities like drought, flood, etc., rather than providing ad hoc or relief measures.

Crop insurance protects farmers' investment in crop production and thus improves their risk bearing capacity. Crop insurance facilitates adoption of improved technologies, encourages higher investment resulting in higher agricultural production.

Crop credit insurance also reduces the risk of becoming defaulter of institutional credit. The reimbursement of indemnities in the case of crop failure enables the farmer to repay his debts and thus, his credit line with the formal financial institutions is maintained intact (Hazell *et al.*, 1986 ; Pomareda, 1986; Mishra, 1996;). The farmers do not have to seek loans from private moneylenders. The farmer does not have to go for distress sale of his produce to repay private debts. Credit insurance ensures repayment of credit, which helps in maintaining the viability of formal credit institutions. The government is relieved from large expenditures incurred for writing-off agricultural loans, providing relief and distress loans etc., in the case of crop failure. A properly designed and implemented crop insurance programme will protect the numerous vulnerable small and marginal farmers from hardship, bring in stability in the farm incomes and increase the farm production (Bhende, 2002).

The farmer is likely to allocate resources in profit maximising way if he is sure that he will be compensated when his income is catastrophically low for reasons beyond his control. A farmer may grow more profitable crops even though they are risky. Similarly, the farmer may adopt improved but uncertain technology when he is assured of compensation in case of failure (Hazell, 1992). This will increase the value added from agriculture, and income of the farm family.

Access and availability of insurance changes the attitude of the farmer, and induces him to take decisions which, otherwise, would not have taken due to aversion to risk. For example, rain-fed paddy was cultivated in one of the riskiest districts i.e., Anuradhapur district of Sri Lanka, for the first time in 1962, as insurance facility was available to the farmers (Ray, 1971).

Income of the farm households from semi-arid tropics engaged predominantly in rain-fed farming was found to be positively associated with the level of risk (Bhende, 2005). Hence, the availability of formal instrument for diffusion of risk like crop insurance will facilitate farmers to adopt risky but remunerative technology and farm activities, resulting in increased income.

Some of the studies confirm the conventional view that moral hazard incentive lead insured farmers to use fewer chemical inputs (Smith and Goodwin, 1996). Babcock and Hennessy (1996), find that at reasonable levels of risk aversion, nitrogen fertiliser and insurance are substitutes, suggesting that those who purchase insurance are likely to decrease nitrogen fertiliser applications. A study by Horowitz and Lichtenberg (1993) find that in the US Midwest, crop insurance exerts considerable influence on maize farmers' chemical use decisions. Those purchasing insurance applies significantly more nitrogen per acre (19 %), spend more on pesticides (21%), and treats more acreage with both herbicides and insecticides (7% and 63%) than those not purchasing insurance. These results suggest that both fertiliser and pesticides may be risk-increasing inputs.

An analysis of data from US agriculture indicates that the producer's first response to risk is to restrict the use of debt. Price support programmes and crop insurance are substitutes in reducing producer risk. The availability of crop insurance in a setting with price supports allows producers to service higher levels of debt with no increase in risk (Atwood *et al.*, 1996).

Efficient risk reducing and loss management strategies such as crop insurance would enable the farmers to take substantial risks without being exposed to hardship. Access to formal risk diffusing mechanisms will induce farmers to maximise returns through adoption of riskier options. Investment in development of groundwater, purchase of exotic breeds for dairy will be encouraged due to insurability of the investment. This will help the individual to augment and increase the farm income (micro perspective), and also help to augment aggregate production in the country (macro perspective). The benefits of crop insurance vary depending on the nature and extent of protection provided by the scheme.

1.4 Credit Linked Insurance

Crop insurance in India is credit linked. Mishra (1994) analysed the impact of a credit-linked comprehensive crop insurance scheme (CCIS) on crop loans, especially to small farmers in Gujarat. It is observed that CCIS had a collateral effect as reflected through the increased loan amount per borrower and reduction in the proportion of non-borrowers among small farmers. The implications of credit expansion are that increased availability of credit can enhance input use, and output and employment that increased share of small farmers in the total loan, can have desirable effects on equity and efficiency considerations.

Though crop insurance is based on area yield, it insures the loan amount. This leads to improved access of small and marginal farmers to institutional credit. In the event of crop failure or drought, loan is repaid in the form of indemnity and thus, there is reduction in the cost of recovery of loans to lending institutions and reduction in the overdue and defaults.

It is observed that insured households invest more on agricultural inputs leading to higher output and income per unit of land. Interestingly, percentage increase in output and income is more for small farms. Based on 1991 data, CCIS was found to contribute 23, 15, and 29 per cent increase in income of insured farmers in Gujarat, Orissa, and Tamil Nadu, respectively (Mishra, 1994).

1.5 Philosophy of Crop Insurance

The generally agreed principles of agricultural insurance are: (1) the uncertainty faced by farmers is transferred to the insurer, and for availing this benefit, the insured farmers pay a risk premium; (2) a large number of participating farmers covering a large area over a period of time enable the horizontal spread of risks over a wide area, and vertical spread over many years; (3) the risk premium reflects the group risk assumed by the insurer; and (4) an indemnity is to be paid to the individual farmer when a loss is incurred due to causes beyond his control, as long as he maintains the insurance contract valid by paying the premium.

First, and basic to the understanding of insurance, is the reality that insurance does not and cannot obliterate risk *per se*. It spreads risk. There are two dimensions to this spread. The first dimension is the spread across an industry or an economy, extended in the case of international reinsurance to the international sphere. The second dimension of spread is through time. Most insurance programmes operate on both dimensions. The important fact to note is that insurance does not directly increase a grower's income. It merely helps manage risks to this income.

Second, insurance is a business. An insurance indemnity only becomes payable in the event of a claim under a policy. The policy must be in force, with premium paid, by the time of the loss event. Most policies incorporate an element of risk sharing, by means of a deductible (also known as an 'excess'). This amount is the percentage of the loss which is borne entirely by the insured.

Third, premium must cover several areas of cost in addition to meeting the cost of paying indemnities under policies in force.

The major role played by insurance programmes is the indemnification of risk-averse individuals who might be adversely affected by natural probabilistic phenomenon. The philosophy of insurance market is based on large numbers where the incidence of risk is distributed over individuals. Insurance, by offering the possibility of shifting risks, enables individuals to engage in risky activities which they would not undertake otherwise (Ahsan *et al.*, 1982).

Individuals cannot influence the nature and occurrence of the risky event. The insurance agency has fairly good but generalised information about the insurer. However, this does not hold true in the case of agriculture or crop insurance. Unlike most other insurance situations, the incidence of crop risk is not independently or randomly distributed among the insured. Good or bad weather may affect the entire population in the area.

Crop insurance is based on the principle of large number. The losses suffered by farmers in a particular locality are borne by farmers in other areas or the reserves accumulated through premiums in good years can be used to pay the indemnities. Thus, a good crop insurance programme combines both self as well as mutual help principle.

1.6 Organisation of the Book

This book looks at the genesis of agricultural insurance in India and discuss various agricultural insurance schemes launched in the country from time to time and the coverage provided by them. The severity of risk is measured by estimating fluctuations in price/yield of different crops at national level and at disaggregate level. The book also look into the role of government in implementing various agricultural insurance schemes and suggest effective agriculture insurance programme for India. The book is organised as follows: Chapter 2 presents and discuss estimates of risk involved in agriculture production at national, state and disaggregate level. Third chapter presents progress and performance of various agriculture insurance schemes launched in India from time to time. It also includes discussion on private sector participation in agriculture insurance. Fourth chapter discusses various issues related to agricultural insurance in India, and also suggests changes in working of various schemes to make them more effective, and to increase their scope and coverage. Ground level experience of agriculture insurance based on micro level investigations in Andhra Pradesh is presented in Chapter 5. Global picture of agriculture insurance is discussed in Chapter 6. Conclusions and policy suggestions are presented in the last chapter.

The book draws material from diverse sources. It uses secondary data published by different government agencies and also draws information from ground level by conducting micro study at household level. Required data on production aspects and prices of selected crops were taken from publications of Central government and state of Andhra Pradesh. Detailed information about crop insurance at the national level were collected from the Agriculture Insurance Company of India Limited (AIC), New Delhi and Report of XIth Plan Working Group on Risk Management in Agriculture, Planning Commission,

Government of India. In order to understand ground level working of national agricultural insurance scheme (NAIS) and insurance products recently launched by some private sectors, a case study was conducted in the state of Andhra Pradesh. This involved survey of farmers who have been covered under NAIS, called beneficiaries and a control sample of farmers who were not covered under the crop insurance, called non-beneficiaries. The main aim of the field survey was to know the perception of beneficiaries and non-beneficiaries of NAIS.

2

Risk in Agricultural Production

In order to develop mechanisms and strategies to mitigate risk in agriculture, it is imperative to understand the magnitude and sources of fluctuations involved in agricultural output. This chapter examines the extent of risk by estimating year to year fluctuations in production of major crops, and also analyses whether the risk in agricultural production declined or increased during the post-reforms period.

The risk associated with crop production is estimated at national level, state level and at disaggregate level. The analysis is extended to district level as there are vast variations in agro climatic conditions across states and districts. The state of Andhra Pradesh was selected to represent disaggregate level. Similarly, various aspects of crop insurance were studied at national level and by undertaking a case study in the state of Andhra Pradesh. This state has a diverse set of crops covered under insurance scheme of government and it is one of the few states where private sector insurance for agriculture is also operating. Initially, new insurance product namely, rainfall insurance was first started in the country in Mahboobnagar district of Andhra Pradesh for castor and groundnut by ICICI Lombard General Insurance Company.

Risk associated with agriculture and various crops was estimated by using instability index as an indicator of risk as below:

$$\text{Instability index} = \text{Standard deviation of natural logarithm } (Y_{t+1}/Y_t).$$

Where, Y_t is the crop area/production/yield/farm harvest prices/gross returns in the current year, and Y_{t+1} represent the same in the next year. This index is unit free and very robust and it measures deviations from the underlying trend (log linear in this case). When there are no deviations from the trend, the ratio Y_{t+1}/Y_t is constant, and thus standard deviation in it is zero. As the series fluctuates more, the ratio of Y_{t+1}/Y_t also fluctuates more, and standard deviation increases. Slightly different variant of this index has been used in the literature before to examine instability and impact of drought on it (Ray, 1983 ; Rao *et al.*, 1988).

This chapter is organised into three sections. The first section examines the extent and change in risk at all India level, the second section discuss state level picture for major crops grown in different states, and the third section deals with disaggregate level picture at district level for the state of Andhra Pradesh.

2.1 All India Picture

Risk revealed by instability index of output, area and productivity of selected crops is presented in Table 2.1.

Table 2.1

Crop-wise Risk in Area, Yield and Output, All India

(Per cent)

Crop	*Area*		*Yield*		*Output*	
	1981-1993	*1993-2004*	*1981-1993*	*1993-2004*	*1981-1993*	*1993-2004*
Rice	4.0	3.1	7.4	8.6	10.9	11.2
Wheat	3.7	3.7	5.8	5.3	7.6	7.5
Groundnut	5.7	3.8	22.0	31.3	25.3	33.2
Rapeseed & Mustard	12.4	12.6	8.0	19.7	16.1	24.7
Cotton	5.8	7.8	15.3	17.9	18.7	19.4
Sugarcane	7.6	6.9	4.0	4.9	8.1	9.1

Among the selected crops, area under rice showed 4 per cent fluctuation around trend during 1980-81 to 1992-93 which declined to 3.1 per cent during post-reform period. Area under wheat also showed almost similar fluctuations but there was no change in extent of fluctuations in area over time. However, there are significant differences in yield and production risk in the two crops. Instability in wheat yield declined from 5.8 per cent in the first period to 5.3 per cent during the second period which also led to small decline in production risk over time. In contrast, risk in rice productivity increased from 7.4 per cent to 8.6 per cent causing increase in production risk from 10.9 per cent during 1980-81 to 1992-93 to 11.25 per cent during 1992-93 to 2003-04.

In the case of groundnut, area followed declining trend after 1992-1993 but fluctuations in area reduced and remained quite low. This narrowing down of production base, made national production and productivity more volatile. Yield risk between the two periods increased from 22 per cent to 31.3 per cent and output risk increased from 25.3 per cent to 33.2 per cent. This made groundnut the most risky crop at national level.

Among all the crops, area under rapeseed/mustard, which is cultivated in *rabi* season, is affected most by vagaries of nature—annual deviation exceeded 12 per cent from trend line. After 1993, fluctuations in rapeseed/mustard yield more than doubled. One reason for this seems to be depression in rapeseed/mustard prices caused by large scale imports of edible oil after 1993-94 through impact on input used in its cultivation. Despite this increase, output of rapeseed/mustard in India fluctuate much less than groundnut.

Cotton crop faced difficult phase due to attack of cotton bollworm during 1997-98 to 2002-03. This affected area more adversely than yield. The net impact on production show only small increase in risk.

Like wheat, risk in area and yield of sugarcane remained low in both the periods but there is small increase in risk in production from 8.1 to 9.1 per cent in production.

These results show that over a period of time, risk in area declined in all the crops except cotton where it showed substantial increase. Yield risk increased in all the crops except wheat which show decline. Year to year fluctuations after 1992-93 remained more or less same in wheat but they showed increase in all other crops. Risk in production is found to be much higher than risk in area. This has implications for farm income. Farmers make only small variation in resource allocated to production, but output or return to their investment follows much larger fluctuations. This causes very high fluctuations in farm income. This brings out the need for undertaking measures to increase irrigation facilities, promote conservation and harvesting of rain water, and evolving crop varieties which are less susceptible to the vagaries of weather to stabilise yield levels (Sharma *et al.*, 2006).

2.2 State Level Picture

Due to large regional diversity in the country, national level picture some time conceals variations across states. Therefore, to understand severity of risk due to fluctuation in crop output at regional level the study uses the state level time series annual data on area, yield and production and area under irrigation for six major crops *viz.*, rice, wheat, groundnut, rapeseed and mustard, cotton and sugarcane for the period 1980-81 to 2003-04. Risk in crop area, production and yield for state level are calculated for two periods: Period I: 1981-82 to 1992-1993 and Period II: 1992-93 to 2003-04. The states have a diversified cropping pattern in different regions depending upon agro-climatic conditions and hence, all the important crops were selected for the present study. Selected crops accounted for more than 80 per cent of the cropped area. The selection of the crops for the study was thus dictated by the availability of data.

Risk in area, production, and yield changes therein for the selected crops for different states are shown in Tables 2.2 to 2.7 along with area under irrigation.

2.2.1 Rice

Comparison across states showed that risk in area is much lower in the states having high rainfall like Bihar, Assam, Orissa, West Bengal, and Eastern Uttar Pradesh. Whereas, risk is found to be very high in states like Andhra Pradesh, Tamil Nadu, Madhya Pradesh, and Gujarat where rainfall is relatively low.

Risk in yield indicate that while high rainfall was very helpful to contain stability in rice area, it was not very helpful in checking fluctuation in yield particularly in the first period. Table 2.2 also shows that expansion of irrigation between the two periods helped in reducing risk in area only in the state of Haryana. In other places

Table 2.2

State-wise Risk in Rice Production and Area under Irrigation

(Per cent)

State	*Period*	*Area*	*Yield*	*Output*	*Irrigated Area*
Andhra Pradesh	1981-1993	11.5	8.6	16.4	94.6
	1993-2004	13.4	9.0	21.0	96.2
Assam	1981-1993	3.4	9.3	12.0	22.4
	1993-2004	3.0	2.4	4.5	14.8
Bihar	1981-1993	7.5	20.3	26.3	35.3
	1993-2004	10.2	15.9	21.6	44.0
Gujarat	1981-1993	10.1	39.6	46.4	49.6
	1993-2004	16.2	35.0	43.5	62.3
Haryana	1981-1993	13.2	8.2	15.9	98.2
	1993-2004	8.0	14.0	11.8	99.7
Jammu & Kashmir	1981-1993	2.9	14.3	14.5	90.5
	1993-2004	4.3	14.4	16.5	90.5
Karnataka	1981-1993	7.6	8.9	15.8	62.0
	1993-2004	21.9	24.4	12.0	64.1
Kerala	1981-1993	3.0	2.7	5.1	39.9
	1993-2004	4.5	5.4	6.7	52.2
Madhya Pradesh	1981-1993	1.6	19.6	20.3	19.3
	1993-2004	33.2	35.5	63.0	22.5
Maharashtra	1981-1993	5.2	18.0	20.4	25.3
	1993-2004	1.2	21.6	21.5	27.8
Orissa	1981-1993	4.0	25.0	28.7	32.7
	1993-2004	3.1	37.1	39.5	37.1
Punjab	1981-1993	4.3	9.4	11.1	98.8
	1993-2004	4.4	5.5	6.5	98.9
Tamil Nadu	1981-1993	12.5	10.6	19.4	91.8
	1993-2004	10.0	15.8	23.2	90.3
Uttar Pradesh	1981-1993	6.5	8.9	14.0	35.8
	1993-2004	6.4	9.6	14.3	64.6
West Bengal	1981-1993	5.1	14.8	17.8	25.9
	1993-2004	5.7	4.9	8.1	39.1

expansion of irrigation hardly influenced year to year fluctuation in area. However, expansion of irrigation helped Bihar, Gujarat, Tamil Nadu, and West Bengal in reducing risk in yield. Risk in yield increased in Andhra Pradesh, Haryana, Karnataka, Kerala, Madhya Pradesh, Maharashtra, Orissa, Tamil Nadu, and Uttar Pradesh despite increase in area of rice under irrigation. It seems that in spite of irrigation progress, rainfall continue to exert very strong influence on year to year fluctuation in rice yield.

Rice production showed very high increase in risk in Andhra Pradesh, Madhya Pradesh, Orissa, and Tamil Nadu. In most of the remaining states production risk shows decline (Table 2.2).

2.2.2 *Wheat*

Gujarat, Jammu and Kashmir, Madhya Pradesh, and Rajasthan show increase in year-to-year fluctuation in area under wheat while remaining states show that wheat area became more stable after 1992-1993. Gujarat, West Bengal, Haryana show remarkable decline in yield instability, whereas, Bihar, Madhya Pradesh, Maharashtra and the hill states show high increase in yield instability (Table 2.3). Like-wise, production instability show sharp decline in Assam, Haryana, Uttar Pradesh, and West Bengal. Year-to-year fluctuation from trend exceeded 50 per cent for Gujarat but remained below 10 per cent in Punjab, Haryana, Uttar Pradesh, and Bihar.

2.2.3 *Groundnut*

Instability in groundnut area was highest in Orissa followed by Rajasthan (Table 2.4). In Orissa, area deviated from the trend by more than 35 per cent while in Rajasthan instability increased to 29.7 per cent after 1993. Tamil Nadu witnessed sharp increase in risk in area, but sharp decline in yield and production. In Gujarat, risk in area is lowest among all the states, but risk in yield and production was highest. Risk in groundnut production and yield exceeded 100 per cent in the state of Gujarat. All the southern states except Andhra Pradesh, Madhya Pradesh, Maharashtra, Orissa, and Uttar Pradesh show decline in risk in yield and production of groundnut.

Table 2.3

State-wise Risk in Wheat Production and Area under Irrigation

(*Per cent*)

State	*Period*	*Area*	*Yield*	*Output*	*Irrigated Area*
Assam	1981-1993	23.3	14.5	21.8	-
	1993-2004	6.9	17.0	16.4	-
Bihar	1981-1993	6.2	4.9	8.5	80.6
	1993-2004	2.1	8.8	9.8	89.4
Gujarat	1981-1993	31.4	32.3	57.5	78.6
	1993-2004	36.7	18.2	50.7	86.6
Haryana	1981-1993	4.5	8.9	10.0	97.0
	1993-2004	3.1	3.8	5.7	98.5
Himachal Pradesh	1981-1993	2.0	28.3	27.5	17.1
	1993-2004	3.1	37.9	38.9	18.6
Jammu & Kashmir	1981-1993	4.3	20.9	19.8	24.3
	1993-2004	6.5	44.1	38.9	25.5
Karnataka	1981-1993	11.9	32.9	33.4	26.7
	1993-2004	7.1	27.1	31.3	39.2
Madhya Pradesh	1981-1993	7.8	7.8	14.4	41.5
	1993-2004	13.3	12.2	24.6	69.5
Maharashtra	1981-1993	16.7	15.9	28.3	54.7
	1993-2004	15.7	20.9	33.7	63.6
Punjab	1981-1993	2.0	8.5	7.8	94.5
	1993-2004	1.5	7.1	7.2	97.1
Rajasthan	1981-1993	12.4	14.3	21.4	87.4
	1993-2004	13.9	15.2	23.7	96.4
Uttar Pradesh	1981-1993	2.8	6.7	8.5	86.3
	1993-2004	1.5	6.4	6.4	92.9
West Bengal	1981-1993	19.6	16.6	19.0	70.9
	1993-2004	6.2	7.4	10.2	78.7

Table 2.4

State-wise Risk in Groundnut Production and Area under Irrigation

(Per cent)

State	*Period*	*Area*	*Yield*	*Output*	*Irrigated Area*
Andhra Pradesh	1981-1993	8.4	21.1	25.4	19.0
	1993-2004	7.9	41.0	47.5	17.4
Gujarat	1981-1993	14.1	119.3	130.9	8.7
	1993-2004	5.4	101.9	101.2	8.1
Karnataka	1981-1993	8.9	36.3	37.2	21.7
	1993-2004	11.3	25.2	33.6	21.4
Madhya Pradesh	1981-1993	12.8	33.8	32.3	3.6
	1993-2004	7.5	29.2	29.9	6.9
Maharashtra	1981-1993	15.6	30.6	33.5	19.5
	1993-2004	7.7	18.7	18.4	30.1
Orissa	1981-1993	36.6	33.6	55.5	21.7
	1993-2004	35.1	20.1	49.9	25.1
Rajasthan	1981-1993	16.9	33.6	26.5	19.9
	1993-2004	29.7	42.2	40.8	34.4
Tamil Nadu	1981-1993	10.7	32.2	33.7	28.1
	1993-2004	15.4	14.7	20.3	29.4
Uttar Pradesh	1981-1993	20.5	33.0	32.8	1.0
	1993-2004	12.1	22.3	26.3	1.4

2.2.4 *Rapeseed and Mustard*

Rapeseed and mustard show lower yield and production risk in most of the states as compared to groundnut (Table 2.5). There is a remarkable improvement in risk in area of rapeseed and mustard after 1993 in the states of Bihar, Haryana, Jammu & Kashmir, Punjab, West Bengal, and Uttar Pradesh. Orissa, Madhya Pradesh, and Gujarat witnessed very high increase in fluctuations in year to year area allocated to rapeseed and mustard. It is ironical that extension of irrigation to rapeseed and mustard did not help in reducing risk in yield and production; rather in most cases it added up to the risk.

Table 2.5

State-wise Risk in Rapeseed and Mustard Production and Area under Irrigation

(Per cent)

State	*Period*	*Area*	*Yield*	*Output*	*Irrigated Area*
Assam	1981-1993	8.2	13.7	14.4	-
	1993-2004	2.5	12.7	13.2	-
Bihar	1981-1993	9.0	29.0	27.8	22.2
	1993-2004	4.3	17.8	18.7	35.1
Gujarat	1981-1993	13.2	24.6	27.4	93.5
	1993-2004	27.5	26.6	40.4	93.0
Haryana	1981-1993	25.0	21.0	32.5	65.0
	1993-2004	12.0	35.4	37.6	71.5
Jammu & Kashmir	1981-1993	18.3	36.9	28.7	76.9
	1993-2004	7.3	41.5	40.6	79.0
Madhya Pradesh	1981-1993	11.1	27.5	32.2	32.1
	1993-2004	22.6	30.4	46.7	38.8
Orissa	1981-1993	56.4	37.2	91.9	14.6
	1993-2004	77.8	98.7	134.5	15.2
Punjab	1981-1993	27.5	11.7	35.5	87.7
	1993-2004	20.3	17.7	23.7	86.7
Rajasthan	1981-1993	24.5	13.7	27.0	63.9
	1993-2004	24.8	22.2	35.7	67.0
Uttar Pradesh	1981-1993	27.0	27.6	16.9	28.6
	1993-2004	15.3	35.1	23.6	56.0
West Bengal	1981-1993	14.2	15.8	21.4	63.5
	1993-2004	9.8	17.9	19.2	69.7

2.2.5 *Cotton*

From the instability in cotton and area under irrigation, it seems that irrigation has very limited impact on risk of both area as well as yield. For instance, Madhya Pradesh and Maharashtra where less than 4 per cent cotton area is irrigated show least risk in area among all the states (Table 2.6). The yield in these states also show almost same risk as in Haryana and Punjab where cotton is grown only under irrigated condition. Probably, attractive alternatives are not available in

Madhya Pradesh and Maharashtra to shift from cotton. Further, yield risk in Punjab and Haryana show increase, whereas it show sharp decrease in Madhya Pradesh and Maharashtra. Lowest yield risk is observed in Karnataka, followed by Tamil Nadu and Andhra Pradesh.

Risk patterns are quite clear in the case of cotton. Maharashtra and Madhya Pradesh have very high risk and low yield. Punjab, Haryana, Gujarat, and Rajasthan also have high risk but this happens at high yield. Southern states exhibit medium yield and more stability.

Table 2.6

State-wise Risk in Cotton Production and Area under Irrigation

(Per cent)

State	*Period*	*Area*	*Yield*	*Output*	*Irrigated Area*
Andhra Pradesh	1981-1993	17.5	29.5	25.8	11.5
	1993-2004	18.8	24.8	27.7	17.4
Gujarat	1981-1993	25.2	50.5	69.5	33.2
	1993-2004	6.6	42.1	43.2	39.6
Haryana	1981-1993	12.8	22.8	20.7	98.8
	1993-2004	9.3	37.1	31.4	99.4
Karnataka	1981-1993	20.2	16.4	26.4	18.1
	1993-2004	18.7	17.2	28.4	19.5
Madhya Pradesh	1981-1993	7.5	50.3	50.1	16.3
	1993-2004	7.2	30.8	31.1	32.8
Maharashtra	1981-1993	4.7	49.6	48.2	3.3
	1993-2004	6.5	35.6	34.9	3.7
Punjab	1981-1993	13.7	32.2	26.8	99.8
	1993-2004	16.9	33.1	34.8	100.0
Rajasthan	1981-1993	9.2	45.9	51.4	91.0
	1993-2004	12.7	51.0	49.5	97.4
Tamil Nadu	1981-1993	14.2	25.6	33.9	40.9
	1993-2004	30.5	18.0	42.9	34.4

2.2.6 Sugarcane

Except the state of Bihar, sugarcane is mostly cultivated under irrigated conditions. Uttar Pradesh, which is the largest producing state show the least risk in area, yield and production (Table 2.7). The other two major sugarcane producing states namely, Tamil Nadu and Maharashtra show sharp rise in risk in sugarcane area as well as in sugarcane production. Punjab represents typical cobweb cycle in sugarcane area and production but yield is quite stable. Production risk in sugarcane show increase in Bihar, Karnataka, Madhya Pradesh, Maharashtra, Orissa, Punjab, and Tamil Nadu but decline at other places. Sugarcane production is most unstable in Orissa, followed by Karnataka and Maharashtra.

Table 2.7

State-wise Risk in Sugarcane Production and Area under Irrigation

(Per cent)

State	*Period*	*Area*	*Yield*	*Output*	*Irrigated Area*
Andhra Pradesh	1981-1993	18.0	14.4	18.4	100.0
	1993-2004	9.6	8.7	12.3	100.0
Assam	1981-1993	7.4	13.4	14.8	-
	1993-2004	5.3	5.3	8.5	-
Bihar	1981-1993	8.7	13.2	17.3	20.6
	1993-2004	9.4	11.5	18.2	25.1
Gujarat	1981-1993	12.5	12.3	10.4	100.0
	1993-2004	10.2	5.5	8.1	100.0
Haryana	1981-1993	13.5	17.1	18.8	94.2
	1993-2004	14.4	6.0	14.5	98.3
Karnataka	1981-1993	7.7	5.6	9.3	99.3
	1993-2004	17.1	15.5	27.4	100.0
Madhya Pradesh	1981-1993	29.7	24.1	13.7	100.0
	1993-2004	25.6	34.5	19.2	100.0
Maharashtra	1981-1993	11.9	12.7	12.9	100.0
	1993-2004	17.7	8.8	23.3	100.0
Orissa	1981-1993	31.3	10.6	39.6	88.3
	1993-2004	37.6	15.1	45.2	100.0
Punjab	1981-1993	15.6	7.2	15.9	92.9
	1993-2004	24.7	6.5	28.8	95.6
Tamil Nadu	1981-1993	9.6	7.3	14.6	100.0
	1993-2004	17.2	11.1	22.9	99.3
Uttar Pradesh	1981-1993	8.1	3.8	8.3	82.5
	1993-2004	5.2	3.6	6.4	89.5

Despite progress of irrigation and improvement in infrastructure and communication, the risk in agriculture production has increased in the country. The risk is much higher for farm income than production, as is evident from lower risk in area and higher risk in production. State-wise results show that only in the states where irrigation is very reliable, it helped in reducing the risk. Those states where irrigation is not very dependable continue to face high risk. In some states farmers face twin problems of very low productivity accompanied by high risk of production. As, with the passage of time, neither technology nor any other variable helped in reducing production risk, particularly in low productivity states, there is a strong need to devise and extend insurance products to agricultural production (Chand and Ramesh, 2007).

2.3 Risk in Andhra Pradesh Agriculture at Disaggregate Level

Variability in agricultural production consists of variability in area and yield, and their interactions. Variation in area under a crop occurs mainly in response to distribution, timelines and amount of rainfall, other climatic factors, expected prices and availability of crop specific inputs. All these factors also affect variations in yield. Further, yield is also affected by outbreak of diseases, pests, and other natural or man-made hazards like flood, drought and fire and many other factors. Different events may affect area and yield in same way or in opposite or different way.

Risk in area, production and yield of rice, cotton and groundnut experienced at state level in Andhra Pradesh during 12 years before and after 1992-93 is presented in Table 2.8. Risk for area shows increase after 1992-93 for rice and cotton and decline in the case of groundnut. It increased from 11.5 to 13.4 in rice and from 17.5 to 18.8 in cotton. In both the periods risk in area was lowest in groundnut. Rice, which is generally grown under irrigated conditions, shows somewhat higher risk in area as compared to groundnut. Area under cotton shows more than double the fluctuations in area under groundnut.

Risk in yield was lower than risk in area in the case of rice, whereas yield of groundnut and cotton show much higher fluctuations than area. The risk of yield did not increase much overtime in the case of rice whereas it almost doubled in the case of groundnut, from 21 to 41, between 1981-1993 and 1993-2004. Despite a lot of concern about susceptibility of cotton to various pests in the recent years, its productivity show less fluctuation after 1993 compared to the period before 1993.

Risk in production of rice was almost double as compared to risk in yield during 1981-1993. In the next 11 years it further increased. In the case of cotton deviations from trend growth in production were lower than that of yield but higher than that of area during 1981-1993. After 1993 production risk in cotton increased despite less unstable yield. Volatility in production of groundnut doubled after 1992-93 and it was as high as 47 per cent in terms of standard deviation from trend. Among the three crops, rice production showed lowest year to year fluctuations.

Besides fluctuation in production, prices received by farmers for their produce are equally important in causing fluctuations in farm income. Therefore, it is important to consider fluctuation in farm income in order to understand and address risk in farm income. It is important to point out that farm harvest prices show much lower fluctuations than fluctuations in yield and production. Second, risk in farm harvest prices show a decline over time in the case of groundnut and cotton, and small increase in the case of rice. Among the three crops, farm harvest prices of rice show lowest instability, 8.3 per cent. The decline in price fluctuations in groundnut and cotton after 1993 seems to be the result of increased integration and improvement taking place in agricultural markets in the country. The reason for small increase in price risk of rice seems to be the result of liberalisation of rice trade after 1995 which was earlier very tightly regulated by the government.

Generally prices and production are expected to have negative covariance as increase in production put downward pressure on price and decrease in production should result in increase in price. This is generally expected to have a smoothening effect on gross return from a crop. But this expectation is met if negative covariance in fluctuations between farm harvest prices and production exceeds variance of either price or production.

Table 2.8

Risk in Area, Production, Yield, Farm Harvest Prices and Gross Revenue from Important Crops in Andhra Pradesh, 1980-81 to 2003-04

(Per cent)

Crop	*Period*	*Area*	*Production*	*Yield*	*FHP*	*GR*
Rice	1980-81 to 1992-93	11.5	16.4	8.6	7.4	21.0
	1992-93 to 2003-04	13.4	21.0	9.0	8.3	19.2
Groundnut	1980-81 to 1992-93	8.4	25.4	21.1	14.3	29.8
	1992-93 to 2003-04	7.9	47.5	41.0	10.8	50.2
Cotton	1980-81 to 1992-93	17.5	25.8	29.5	23.9	37.9
	1992-93 to 2003-04	18.8	27.7	24.8	22.5	37.9

Note: FHP—Farm Harvest Price; GR—Gross Returns.

Price instability though shows decline in groundnut and cotton over time, it still rules very high in the case of cotton. The net effect of fluctuations in production and prices on farm income represented by gross returns show that instability in area, production, yield and prices do not negate each other. Rather, their impact get accumulated to some degree because of which risk in farm income is found higher than risk in area, production and prices in all the cases, and this has not changed over time.

2.3.1 *Risk at District Level for the State of Andhra Pradesh*

In order to find out whether risk in agriculture at disaggregate level presents a different picture than that at aggregate level, risk in selected dimensions was estimated for each district in the state of Andhra Pradesh. Rather than presenting risk results for each of the districts in Andhra Pradesh, these estimates are presented in terms of range and frequency of decline, increase or no significant change between the two periods selected for the study. These results are then compared with results revealed by aggregate data at state level.

Risk in rice area at state level of Andhra Pradesh was 11.5 per cent during 1981-1993 and 13.4 per cent during 1993 to 2004. At district level it ranged from 7 to 60 per cent in the first period and from 11 to 44 per cent in the second period. In groundnut, district level risk in area ranged from 9 to 54 per cent and 8 to 50 per cent in the two periods against state level risk of 8.4 and 7.9 per cent. Area in the cotton exhibit risk in the range of 6 to 89 per cent and 7 to 67 per cent in the two periods. There is not only wide variation in risk across districts, in some cases range of risk at district level narrowed down in contrast to increase in risk at state level. Similar pattern is observed in the case of production, yield, farm harvest prices, and gross returns. In some cases risk shown by state aggregate is found lower than the minimum value in the range of risk across districts. These results indicate that in a large state like Andhra Pradesh state level estimate of risk involved in agriculture production, prices and return highly under estimate risk at disaggregate level. These state level estimates provide indication of shock in supply or agriculture output at aggregate level but they completely conceal the volatility to which sub-region is subjected.

Table 2.9

Range of Risk in Area, Production, Yield, Farm Harvest Prices and Gross Revenue at Disaggregate Level

(Per cent)

Crop	*Period*	*Area*	*Production*	*Yield*	*FHP*	*GR*
Rice	I	7 to 60	16 to 86	9 to 43	7 to 18	20 to 79
Rice	II	11 to 44	16 to 67	11 to 46	6 to 18	19 to 70
Groundnut	I	9 to 54	14 to 62	10 to 47	7 to 22	15 to 64
Groundnut	II	8 to 50	18 to 83	15 to 75	9 to 19	17 to 82
Cotton	I	6 to 89	32 to 139	37 to 137	20 to 86	45 to 154
Cotton	II	7 to 67	32 to 90	18 to 63	16 to 43	34 to 99

Note: Period I and II indicate years 1981-1993 and 1993-2004, respectively.

District level risk estimates show that range of risk in production and gross returns narrowed down for rice and cotton but it has widened for groundnut.

Another way to examine appropriateness of state level estimates of risk to reflect changes at district level is to compare changes in risk over time at state level with changes at district level. This is accomplished in Table 2.10. The Table shows per cent distribution of districts in Andhra Pradesh which have seen significant increase or decrease in risk in area, production, yield, farm harvest prices, and gross revenue, and those which did not see significant change in the level of risk. The significant change is defined as change of more than one percentage point.

This shows that for rice 32 per cent districts witnessed decline in risk in area, 36 per cent witnessed decline in production fluctuations, and 45 per cent witnessed decline in risk in yield, whereas, state level estimates show only increase in risk. Similarly, in groundnut compared to increase at state level, only half of the districts show increase in risk in gross returns. State level data indicate decline in risk in cotton yield but district level data indicate increase in as much as 17 per cent of the districts of the state. The most striking variation in state and district level data is found in the case of risk in gross returns from cotton which shows no change at state level but declined in the case of 83 per cent districts.

Table 2.10

Distribution of District based on Significant Change in Level of Risk

Category	Crop	Area	Production	Yield	FHP	Gross Returns
A. Districts experienced increase in risk (%)	Rice	59.1	59.1	40.9	27.3	27.3
	Groundnut	54.6	68.2	59.1	13.6	50.0
	Cotton	11.1	33.3	16.7	5.6	16.7
B. Districts experienced decrease in risk (%)	Rice	31.8	36.4	45.5	54.5	72.7
	Groundnut	40.9	31.8	36.4	72.8	40.9
	Cotton	72.2	66.7	83.3	88.8	83.3
C. Districts experienced change less than one percentage point (%)	Rice	9.1	4.5	13.6	18.2	0
	Groundnut	4.5	0	4.5	13.6	9.1
	Cotton	16.7	0	0	5.6	0

2.3.2 *Factors Affecting Risk*

Factors that have affected risk overtime vary from crop to crop. The main reason for increase in risk of cotton area and production after 1992-93 seems to be extension of cotton cultivation to non-traditional areas where cotton has replaced *jowar*, pulses and other cereal crops. Cotton cultivation has been extended to red *chalka* soils which are not quite suitable for cotton cultivation.

The major source of increase in risk and its high level in groundnut yield is frequent and severe droughts during the period II, that is, from 1992-93 to 2003-04. In 8 out of 11 years, successive droughts were reported in Anantapur and their neighbouring districts which are major groundnut growing areas. In one year excessive rains caused the failure of crop in two or three districts. Further, decline in area under irrigation also contributed to the increase in yield instability. Groundnut producers suffered not only due to increase in year to year fluctuations but they also harvested lower yield in the second period.

Table 2.11

Factors Related to Risk in Andhra Pradesh

Crop	*Period*	*Area ('000 ha)*	*Yield (kg/ha)*	*Irrigated Area %*
Rice	I	3757	2208	94.64
	II	3657	2713	96.11
Groundnut	I	1892	877	19.01
	II	1972	869	17.31
Cotton	I	562	255	11.48
	II	957	284	17.42

Note: Period I and II indicate years 1981-1993 and 1993-2004, respectively.

Increase in risk in rice area and production seems mainly due to erratic, irregular and insufficient power supply for irrigation purpose, and more erratic rainfall distribution during the period II. In the case of cotton, expansion in irrigation seems to have lowered yield instability but not area and production risk.

Despite progress of irrigation and other infrastructure supporting agriculture, the risk in agricultural production show increase after early 1990s in major crops grown in Andhra Pradesh. In contrast to this, farm harvest prices of groundnut and cotton show a decline in risk during 1993 to 2004 as compared to 1981 to 1993. More than half to 89 per cent districts witnessed decline in price fluctuations. The results of the study indicate that in a large state like Andhra Pradesh, picture of risk as seen in state level data may turn out to be vastly different than what is experienced at disaggregate level. In some cases state level estimate may be completely misleading as seen in the case of risk in cotton production which show increase at state level but decrease in two-third districts. The effect of technology in stabilising yield varies across districts. Yield variability in cotton declined in more than 80 per cent of the districts after 1993 despite increase in rainfall deviations. Among the three crops selected for the study, groundnut has turned the most risky crop in respect of production as well as gross returns.

The net effect of fluctuations in production and prices on farm income show that risk in area, production, yield and prices do not negate each other. Risk in farm income is found higher than risk in area, production and prices in all the cases, and this has not changed over time. This underscores the need for addressing risk in farm income by devising area-specific crop insurance or other suitable mechanisms.

3

Progress and Performance of Agricultural Insurance

The question of introducing an agriculture insurance scheme was examined soon after the Independence in 1947. Following an assurance given in this regard by the then Ministry of Food and Agriculture (MOFA) in the Central Legislature to introduce crop and cattle insurance, a special study was commissioned during 1947-48 to consider whether insurance should follow an 'individual approach' or a 'homogenous area approach'. The study favoured 'homogenous area approach' even as various agro-climatically homogenous areas are treated as a single unit and the individual farmers in such cases pay the same rate of premium and receive the same benefits, irrespective of their individual fortunes. In 1965, the government introduced a Crop Insurance Bill and circulated a model scheme of crop insurance on a compulsory basis to state governments for their views. The bill provided for the Central government to frame a reinsurance scheme to cover indemnity obligations of the states. However, none of the states favoured the scheme because of the financial obligations involved in it. On receiving the reactions of the state governments, the subject was referred to an Expert Committee headed by the then Chairman, Agricultural Price Commission, in July 1970 for full examination of the economic, administrative, financial, and actuarial implications of the subject.

3.1 Crop Insurance Approaches

It is important to mention in the beginning that crop insurance is based on either area approach or individual approach. Area approach is based on 'defined areas' which could be a district, a *taluk*, a block/ a *mandal*, or any other smaller contiguous area. The indemnity limit originally was 80 per cent, which was changed to 60 per cent, 80 per cent, and 90 per cent corresponding to high, medium and low risks areas. The actual average yield/hectare for the defined area is determined on the basis of crop cutting experiments (CCEs). These CCEs are the same conducted as part of the general crop estimation survey (GCES) in various states. If the actual yield in CCEs of an insured crop for the defined area falls short of the specified guaranteed yield or threshold yield, all the insured farmers growing that crop in the area are entitled for claims. The claims are calculated using the formula:

$$\frac{\text{(Guaranteed Yield - Actual Yield)}}{\text{(Guaranteed Yield)}} * \text{Sum Insured of the Farmer}$$

The claims are paid to the credit institutions in the case of loanee farmers and to the individuals who insured their crops in the other cases. The credit institution would adjust the amount against the crop loan and pay the residual amount, if any, to the farmer. Area yield insurance is practically an all-risk insurance. This is very important for developing countries with a large number of small farms. However, there are delays in compensation payments.

In the case of individual approach, assessment of loss is made separately for each insured farmer. It could be for each plot or for the farm as a whole (consisting of more than one plot at different locations). Individual farm-based insurance is suitable for high-value crops grown under standard practices. Liability is limited to cost of cultivation. This type of insurance provides for accurate and timely compensation. However, it involves high administrative costs.

Weather index insurance has similar advantages to those of area yield insurance. This programme provides timely compensation made on the basis of weather index, which is usually accurate. All communities whose incomes are dependent on the weather can buy this insurance. A basic disadvantage could arise due to changing weather patterns and poor density of weather stations.

Weather insurance helps ill-equipped economies deal with adverse weather conditions (65% of Indian agriculture is dependent on natural factors, especially rainfall. Drought is another major problem that farmers face). It is a solution to financial problems brought on by adverse weather conditions. This insurance covers a wide section of people and a variety of crops; its operational costs are low; transparent and objective calculation of weather index ; and quick settlement of claims.

3.2 Agricultural Insurance Schemes

3.2.1 First Individual Approach Scheme 1972-1978

Different forms of experiments on agricultural insurance on a limited, ad hoc and scattered scale started from 1972-73 when the General Insurance Corporation (GIC) of India introduced a crop Insurance Scheme on H-4 cotton. In the same year, general insurance business was nationalised and, GIC of India was set up by an Act of Parliament. The new corporation took over the experimental scheme in respect of H-4 cotton. This scheme was based on 'individual approach' and later included groundnut, wheat, and potato. The scheme was implemented in the states of Andhra Pradesh, Gujarat, Karnataka, Maharashtra, Tamil Nadu, and West Bengal. It continued up to 1978-79 and covered only 3110 farmers for a premium of Rs.4.54 lakhs against claims of Rs.37.88 lakhs.

3.2.2 Pilot Crop Insurance Scheme (PCIS) 1979-1984

In the background and experience of the aforesaid experimental scheme, a study was commissioned by the GIC of India and entrusted to Prof. V.M. Dandekar to suggest a suitable approach to be followed in the scheme. The recommendations of the study were accepted and a pilot crop insurance scheme (PCIS) was launched by the GIC in 1979, which was based on 'area approach' for providing insurance cover against a decline in crop yield below the threshold level. The scheme covered cereals, millets, oilseeds, cotton, potato, and chickpea, and it was confined to loanee farmers of institutional sources on a voluntary basis. The premium paid was shared between the GIC of India and state governments in the ratio of 2:1. The maximum sum insured was 100 per cent of the crop loan, which was later increased to 150 per cent. The insurance premium ranged from 5 to 10 per cent of the sum insured. Premium charges payable by small/marginal farmers were subsidised by 50 per cent shared equally between the state and Central governments. PCIS–1979 was implemented in 12 states till 1984-85 and covered 6.23 lakh farmers for a premium of Rs.195.01 lakhs against claims of Rs.155.68 lakhs in the entire period. The details about the coverage, in terms of number of farmers, area covered, premium collected and total claims paid for the PCIS implemented during 1979 through 1984-85 have been presented in Table 3.1.

Table 3.1

Performance of Pilot Crop Insurance Scheme during 1979-80 to 1984-85

Particulars	*1979-80*	*1980-81*	*1981-82*	*1982-83*	*1983-84*	*1984-85*	*Total*
Number of states	3	3	8	9	11	12	-
Area covered (ha)	13181	18703	24467	70729	87347	477333	691760
Farmers covered	16265	23442	24625	50855	60349	447086	622622
Sum insured (Rs.lakh)	130.30	165.77	202.82	468.26	653.64	4446.49	6067.28
Premium Collected (Rs.lakh)	5.53	6.93	7.55	15.65	21.15	138.20	195.01
Claims paid (Rs.lakh)	5.29	3.27	9.64	37.32	8.37	91.80	155.68
Claim's ratio (%)	95.71	47.10	127.67	238.46	39.56	66.42	79.83

Source: Tripathi, 1987.

The overall claim to premium ratio was 79.83 per cent indicating that about 79.83 per cent of the total premium collections were used for the payment of claims or indemnities. The average premium collected for crop insurance declined from Rs.41.95 per hectare in 1979-80 to Rs.22.13 per hectare during 1982-83 and increased thereafter to Rs.28.95 per hectare in 1984-85. Incidentally, the average premium collected per hectare was the lowest and the average indemnity paid per insured crop hectare was the highest (Rs.52.76 per insured hectare) during 1982-83.

Following were some of the shortcomings that impinged upon the coverage of the crop insurance scheme:

- Since crop insurance was linked to crop loans, many small and marginal farmers could not participate in the crop insurance scheme because a majority of these farms have poor access to institutional credit.
- The unit of insurance was very large.
- Lack of awareness among the farmers about the crop insurance scheme.
- Major commercial crops like cotton and sugarcane were excluded from the crop insurance scheme.

3.2.3 Comprehensive Crop Insurance Scheme (CCIS) 1985-1999

This scheme was linked to short term credit and was implemented based on the 'homogenous area approach'. Till *kharif* 1999, the scheme was adopted in 15 states and 2 UTs. Both PCIS and CCIS were confined only to farmers who borrowed seasonal agricultural loan from financial institutions. The main distinguishing feature of the two schemes was that PCIS was on voluntary basis whereas CCIS was compulsory for loanee farmers in the participating states/UTs. Main features of the scheme were:

1. It covered farmers availing crop loans from financial institutions, for growing food crops and oilseeds, on compulsory basis. The coverage was restricted to 100 per cent of the crop loan subject to a maximum of Rs.10,000 per farmer.
2. The premium rates were 2 per cent for cereals and millets, and 1 per cent for pulses and oilseeds. Farmers' share of premium was collected at the time of disbursement of loan. Half of the premium payable by small and marginal farmers was subsidised equally by the Central and state governments.(Tripathi, 1987).
3. Burden of premium and claims was shared by Central and state governments in a 2:1 ratio.
4. The scheme was a multi-agency effort, involving GoI, state governments, banking institutions and GIC.

CCIS was implemented till *kharif* 1999 and it covered 763 lakh farmers for a premium of Rs. 404 crores against claims of Rs.2303 crores. As can be seen from Table 3.2, the benefits of CCIS were highly skewed towards Gujarat, as more than half (58%) of the total indemnities under CCIS were paid to groundnut farmers in this state alone. The other participating states which contributed 84 per cent of the premium during 1985-1999 received only 42 per cent of total claims. The claim-premium ratio was nearly 20.74 for Gujarat, while it was only about 5.72 at the all India level. Saurashtra experienced severe drought during 1985, 1986 and 1987. Large scale crop failures (especially groundnut in *kharif*) were reported during 1990, 1991 and 1993. This resulted in very high indemnity payments. There were reports indicating that the farmers used to pressurise village level officials conducting crop cutting experiments to underestimate the crop yields so that farmers in the area could get the indemnity payments (Mishra, 1994).

Table 3.2

State-wise CCIS Performance during 1985–1999

State	*Premium Collected*		*Claims*		*Claim-Premium Ratio*
	Rs. Crores	*% Share*	*Rs. Crores*	*% Share*	
Gujarat	64.45	16	1336.93	58	20.74
Maharashtra	60.42	15	253.33	11	4.19
Andhra Pradesh	100.70	25	322.70	14	3.20
Other states	177.24	44	3918.60	17	2.21
India	402.81	100	2305.04	100	5.72

Source: Agriculture Insurance Company of India (AIC) Limited, New Delhi.

Among crops, groundnut has the highest loss cost of 16.02 per cent. Furthermore, groundnut accounts for 53 per cent of the total indemnity though its share in the premium was only 19 per cent. All India loss cost was 9.29 per cent, and among crop groups, cereals posted lower cost with 6.6 per cent (Table 3.3).

The major shortcomings of the scheme were area approach, coverage confined to loanee farmers, uniform premium rate for all the farmers and regions, coverage of few crops, and time lag for indemnity payment (Jain, 2004).

Table 3.3

Crop-wise CCIS Performance during 1985–1999

Crop	*Premium (%)*	*Claims (%)*	*Claims to Premium Ratio*	*Claims as % of Sum Assured*
Paddy	57.88	31.38	3.12	6.24
Wheat	4.42	1.30	1.69	3.39
Jowar	8.35	4.96	3.42	6.83
Bajra	4.12	5.40	7.53	15.06
Other cereals	1.39	0.66	2.69	5.38
All cereals	76.16	43.70	3.30	6.60
Groundnut	19.00	52.94	16.02	16.02
Other oilseeds	3.51	1.40	2.28	2.28
All oilseeds	22.51	54.34	13.88	13.88
Pulses	1.33	1.96	8.50	8.50
All crops	100	100	5.75	9.29

Source: Agricultural Insurance Company of India (AIC) Limited, New Delhi.

3.2.4 *Experimental Crop Insurance Scheme (ECIS) 1997-98*

As demanded by various states from time to time, attempts were made to modify the existing CCIS. During 1997, a new scheme, namely Experimental Crop Insurance Scheme was introduced during *rabi* 1997-98 season with the intention to cover even those small and marginal farmers who do not borrow from institutional sources. This scheme was implemented in 14 districts of 5 states. The scheme provided 100 per cent subsidy on premium. The premium and claims were shared by Central and state governments in 4:1 ratio. The scheme covered 4.78 lakh farmers for a sum insured of Rs.172 crores and the claims paid were Rs.39.78 crores against a premium of Rs.2.86 crores. The scheme was discontinued after one season and based on its experience National Agricultural Insurance Scheme (NAIS) was started.

3.2.5 *National Agricultural Insurance Scheme (NAIS) 1999*

The National Agricultural Insurance Scheme (NAIS) was introduced in the country from the *rabi* season of 1999-2000. Agricultural Insurance Company of India Ltd. (AIC), which was incorporated in December 2002, and started operating from April 2003, took over the implementation of NAIS. This scheme is available to both loanees and non-loanees. It covers all food grains, oilseeds, and annual horticultural/commercial crops for which past yield data are available for an adequate number of years. Among the annual commercial and horticultural crops, sugarcane, potato, cotton, ginger, onion, turmeric, chillies, coriander, cumin, jute, tapioca, banana, and pineapple are covered under the scheme. The scheme is operating on the basis of both 'area approach', for widespread calamities, and 'individual approach', for localised calamities such as hailstorm, landslide, cyclone, and floods.

The premium rates applicable on the sum insured are:

Bajra and oilseeds	:	3.5 %
Other *kharif* crops	:	2.5 %
Wheat	:	1.5 %
Other *rabi* crops	:	2.0 %

Annual commercial/horticultural crops: Actuarial rate

Initially, the premium in the case of small and marginal farmers was subsidised at 50 per cent, which was shared equally by the Government of India and the concerned state/UT. The premium subsidy was to be phased out over a period of five years, at present 10 per cent subsidy is provided on the premium payable by small and marginal farmers.

Coverage of NAIS: Country Level

Initially, only nine states/UTs participated in the NAIS. It covered 5.8 lakh farmers and 7.8 lakh hectares of cropped area (Table 3.4). The coverage under NAIS increased dramatically after the *kharif* 2000. The number of farmers increased from 84.1 lakhs in *kharif* 2000 to 129.3 lakhs by *kharif* 2006, and the area coverage reached 196.7 lakh hectares from 132.2 lakh hectares during this period. The coverage has been far larger during the *kharif* than *rabi* seasons. In seven *kharif* seasons, since *kharif* 2000, a total of 73.14 million farmers have been covered, as against 23.94 million farmers in the eight *rabi* seasons since *rabi* 1999-2000. The trend in *kharif* coverage appears to be linked to the expansion of participating states, crops notified, extent of drought, and non-borrower farmers' decision to participate in the scheme. Non-borrower farmers generally opted for crop insurance only

Table 3.4

Season-wise Performance of the National Agricultural Insurance Scheme

S. No.	*Season*	*No. of Covered States/UTs*	*Farmers Covered (lakhs)*	*Area (lakh ha)*	*Sum Assured (Rs. Crore)*	*Premium (Rs. Crore)*	*Total Claims (Rs. Crore)*
	Rabi						
1.	1999-2000	9	5.8	7.8	356	5	8
2.	2000-01	18	20.9	31.1	1603	28	59
3.	2001-02	20	19.6	31.5	1498	30	65
4.	2002-03	21	23.3	40.4	1838	39	189
5.	2003-04	22	44.2	64.7	3050	64	497
6.	2004-05	23	35.3	53.4	3774	76	161
7.	2005-06	23	40.5	72.2	5072	105	338
8.	2006-07	23	49.8	76.3	6593	143	477
Sub Total			**239.4**	**377.4**	**23784**	**490**	**1794**
	Kharif						
1.	2000	17	84.1	132.2	6903	207	1222
2.	2001	20	87.0	128.9	7503	262	494
3.	2002	21	97.7	155.3	9432	326	1824
4.	2003	23	79.7	123.6	8114	283	653
5.	2004	25	126.9	242.7	13171	459	1038
6.	2005	25	126.7	205.3	13517	450	1060
7.	2006	25	129.3	196.7	14759	467	1772
Sub Total			**731.4**	**1184.7**	**73399**	**2454**	**8063**
	Sum (kharif +rabi)						
1.	1999-2000	9	5.8	7.8	356	5	8
2.	2000-01	18	105.0	163.3	8506	235	1281
3.	2001-02	20	106.6	160.4	9001	292	559
4.	2002-03	21	121.0	195.7	11270	365	2013
5.	2003-04	23	123.9	188.3	11164	347	1150
6.	2004-05	25	162.2	296.1	16945	535	1199
7.	2005-06	25	167.2	277.5	18589	555	1398
8.	2006-07	25	179.1	273.0	21352	610	2249
Grand Total			**970.8**	**1562.1**	**97183**	**2944**	**9857**

Source: Economic Survey (2007-08) and AIC (2008).

selectively, after being almost certain of crop failure.[1] During the entire period from 1999-2000 through 2006-07, the NAIS covered 97.08 million farmers and 156.21 million hectares area. The total sum insured during *kharif* and *rabi* seasons taken together was to the tune of Rs. 97183 crores and the premium collected was Rs. 2944 crores (Table 3.4). The average premium charged during *kharif* was Rs. 3.34 per hundred rupees of sum insured as against Rs. 2.06 per hundred rupees of sum insured in the *rabi* season. The average premium rate of Rs. 3.03 indicates the dominance of risky crops in the crop area insured during the *kharif* season.

To have a clear picture of penetration of NAIS in each season, we related the number of holdings (farmers) covered to the total number of holdings. In the first season, i.e., *rabi* 1999-2000, only 0.5 per cent of the holdings were covered by NAIS (Table 3.5) and this proportion has been slowly going up since then. It reached 4.31 per cent in *rabi*

Table 3.5

Season-wise Share of Insured Farmers in Total Holdings and Area

(Per cent)

Crop Year	*Rabi*		*Kharif*		*Total*	
	Holdings	*Area*	*Holdings*	*Area*	*Holdings*	*Area*
1999-2000	0.50	0.41	-	-	0.50	0.41
2000-01	1.81	1.66	7.28	7.07	9.09	8.73
2001-02	1.70	1.65	7.53	6.77	9.23	8.42
2002-03	2.02	2.30	8.46	8.82	10.48	11.12
2003-04	3.83	3.39	6.90	6.48	10.73	9.88
2004-05	3.06	2.80	10.99	12.73	14.04	15.53
2005-06	3.51	3.79	10.97	10.77	14.45	14.56
2006-07	4.31	4.02	11.19	10.32	15.51	14.32

Source: Authors' calculations based on data taken from *Agricultural Statistics at a Glance* (2007), and *Economic Survey* (2007-08) and AIC (2008).

1. In *kharif* a farmer can go for insurance during April 1 to June 30. In states like Andhra Pradesh, some indication of monsoon becomes available around that time. Based on the subjective assessment about rainfall and consequent impact on crop, farmers opted for crop insurance if they expected severe damage to crop and were sure to get insurance claim. The phenomenon is often referred to as "adverse selection" in technical parlance.

2006-07. In the first *kharif* season of 2000, more than 7 per cent of the holdings in the country were provided insurance cover for some crop(s). This has been going up and touched 11.19 per cent in *kharif* 2006. The same is more or less true for area coverage as well. It is also noteworthy that except some years, the percentage of holdings covered was higher than the percentage of area covered, suggesting a higher penetration among small holdings (Raju and Chand, 2008).

From 1999-2000 to 2006-07, the scheme covered 9-16 per cent farmers, 8-16 per cent crop area, and 2.28-3.77 per cent of crop output in value terms in different years (Table 3.6). The amount of claims was much higher than the premium paid, indicating loss in the operation of this scheme. During 2000-01 and 2002-03, the claims were more than five times of the premium paid. During 2003-04 and 2004-05, the amount of claims was more than double of the premium collected. As claims exceeded premiums, there was a net loss in the scheme, even without considering the administrative cost. The magnitude of loss can also be seen by comparing the ratio of 'claims to sum assured' with ratio of 'premium to sum assured'. During the year 2005-06, claims constituted 7.52 per cent as against 2.97 per cent premium on the sum assured (Table 3.6). This implies a loss of 4.55 per cent of the assured value of output.

Table 3.6

Year-wise Performance of National Agricultural Insurance Scheme

Year	*Sum Assured as % of Value of Crop Output*	*Claims Ratio (Claims/ Premium)*	*Premium/ Sum Assured %*	*Claims/ Sum Assured %*	*Ratio of Borrower and Non-borrower Insured Farmers*
2000-01	2.28	5.45	2.76	15.06	97:3
2001-02	2.22	1.91	3.24	6.20	93:7
2002-03	2.92	5.52	3.23	17.84	86:14
2003-04	2.46	3.29	3.11	10.22	75:25
2004-05	3.77	2.24	3.16	7.06	88:12
2005-06	3.76	2.53	2.97	7.52	85:15

Source: Authors' calculations based on the data taken from *Economic Survey* (2007-08), *National Accounts Statistics* (2007) and AIC (2007).

In the beginning, only 3 per cent non-borrowers adopted crop insurance offered under NAIS. At present, the proportion of non-borrowers in the scheme is 15 per cent (Table 3.6). This shows that the scheme is operational mainly because farmers availing loan from institutional sources are required to go for insurance, irrespective of the fact whether they are interested in it or not.

The number of loanee farmers covered under NAIS averaged around 19 lakh in the *rabi* season during 2000-01 and 2002-03. This number showed a significant increase during the next three *rabi* seasons (2003-04 to 2005-06) and reached the figure of 32.75 lakh. The number of non-borrower farmers showed wide year-to-year fluctuations. There was a big jump in the non-loanee farmers opting for insurance in the year after 2002-03 which was a very severe drought year. The compensation received by those who had insured, induced a large number of farmers to take benefit of insurance in the adverse event. This shows a strong tendency towards adverse selection problem. Further, the non-borrower farmers' participation had come from those areas and crops, which were most likely to report high crop losses. Their participation was predictably the highest, during adverse seasons. Based on the coverage between 1999-2000 and 2005-2006, the loss cost to NAIS for non-borrower farmers was a staggering 27 per cent, compared to 9 per cent for the loanee farmers.

State Level Coverage of NAIS

As stated earlier, only nine states participated in NAIS during 1999 *rabi* season. In 2006-07, the NAIS is being implemented by all the states except Punjab and Arunachal Pradesh, Manipur, Mizoram, and Nagaland. Since the beginning of the scheme till the *rabi* season of 2006-07, 97.08 million cases were extended the insurance cover. Out of these, 19.5 per cent were in Maharashtra, 15.4 per cent in Andhra Pradesh, 13.2 per cent in Madhya Pradesh, and 8.4 per cent each in Gujarat and Uttar Pradesh. Thus, these five states accounted for 65 per cent of the total cases and 69 per cent of area insured under NAIS. It is pertinent to mention that share of these states in all-India holdings and all-India cropped area is 8.5 per cent and 9.2 per cent, respectively.

The proportion of beneficiaries receiving indemnity payments ranged from zero in Jammu & Kashmir to 67 per cent of the participating farmers in Jharkhand (Table 3.7). The percentage of insured cases who got claims was the highest in Himachal Pradesh (60%), followed by Karnataka (47%), Bihar (42%), Tamil Nadu (36%), Gujarat (35%), Maharashtra (30%), and Chhattisgarh (28%).

Table 3.7

State-wise Distribution of Insurance Cases, Area and Claim to Premium Ratio under NAIS

States	*Share in Cases Insured %*	*Share in Area under Insured %*	*Insurance Cases Received Claims %*	*Premium/ Sum Insured %*	*Claims/ Sum Insured %*	*Claim/ Premium Ratio*
Andhra Pradesh	15.41	14.37	19.69	2.76	7.30	2.65
Assam	0.09	0.04	12.26	2.51	2.18	0.87
Bihar	1.72	1.18	42.40	2.18	25.05	11.51
Chhattisgarh	4.41	5.89	27.61	2.59	8.66	3.34
Goa	0.01	0.01	13.94	1.76	1.12	0.63
Gujarat	8.41	12.58	35.08	4.43	16.68	3.76
Haryana	0.37	0.28	8.34	3.16	0.84	0.27
Himachal Pradesh	0.14	0.05	59.56	2.29	9.64	4.21
Jammu & Kashmir	0.01	0.01	0.00	1.88	0.00	0.00
Jharkhand	1.26	0.43	67.13	2.43	30.76	12.67
Karnataka	7.31	7.23	46.58	3.25	16.06	4.94
Kerala	0.29	0.15	19.29	2.09	5.62	2.69
Madhya Pradesh	13.16	21.77	22.91	3.05	5.42	1.78
Maharashtra	19.47	12.56	29.71	3.63	8.47	2.33
Meghalaya	0.01	0.01	10.63	6.32	2.96	0.47
Orissa	7.96	4.99	21.86	2.53	7.13	2.82
Rajasthan	5.50	8.16	23.95	2.77	8.05	2.90
Sikkim	0.00	0.00	8.60	1.01	1.09	1.08
Tamil Nadu	0.86	0.90	35.80	2.07	13.25	6.40
Tripura	0.01	0.00	17.24	2.88	1.91	0.66
Uttar Pradesh	8.46	7.71	20.50	1.96	3.27	1.67
Uttaranchal	0.04	0.03	18.45	1.56	1.15	0.73
West Bengal	5.09	1.63	14.66	2.60	3.98	1.53
Andaman & Nicobar	0.00	0.00	5.60	2.32	0.69	0.30
Pondicherry	0.02	0.02	22.09	1.97	4.70	2.39
Total (India)	100	100	27.02	3.08	9.55	3.10

Source: Authors' calculations based on data taken from AIC (2007).

The farmers claiming indemnity payment accounted for 67.3 per cent of the total 21.34 million beneficiaries (recipient of claims) in Andhra Pradesh, Gujarat, Karnataka, Madhya Pradesh, and Maharashtra. The claim–premium ratio was less than unity in Assam, Goa, Haryana, Jammu and Kashmir, Meghalaya, Tripura, Uttaranchal, and Andaman and Nicobar Islands, implying no loss in premium received by NAIS in these states. Bihar and Jharkhand were on the other extreme, where claims paid by NAIS were more than ten times of the premium collected. In Tamil Nadu and Karnataka, the claims paid by the scheme were 6.4 and 4.9 times, respectively of the premiums obtained (Table 3.7).

On an average, 1.63 ha area was insured per farmer under NAIS during *rabi* 1999 through *rabi* 2005-06. However, the average area insured per participating farmer varied across the states. It was around half a hectare in the states of Himachal Pradesh, Jharkhand, Tripura, and West Bengal, whereas it was more than the national average of 1.63 ha/farmer in the states of Chhattisgarh, Gujarat, Madhya Pradesh, Rajasthan, and Tamil Nadu (Table 3.8). The average sum insured per household ranged from less than Rs. 5000 in Goa, Himachal Pradesh, and Jharkhand to more than Rs. 15000 in Gujarat, Tamil Nadu, and Pondicherry. The average amount insured per farmer under NAIS at the aggregate level was Rs. 9573. Similarly, the average sum insured was Rs. 5860/ha and it varied from less than Rs. 3000/ha in Chhattisgarh, Goa, and Madhya Pradesh to more than Rs. 15000/ha in Tripura.

The average premium paid by the individual farmer ranged from Rs. 71 in Goa to Rs. 781 in Gujarat, while on per hectare basis it varied between Rs. 44 (Goa) and Rs. 513 (Meghalaya). The average amount of indemnity claimed varied from less than Rs. 100 per farmer in Goa, Haryana, Jammu & Kashmir, and Andaman and Nicobar Islands to more than Rs. 1500 per participating farmer in Karnataka (Rs. 1691), Tamil Nadu (Rs. 2135), Bihar (Rs. 2873), and Gujarat (Rs. 2938). The average claims or indemnities per hectare varied from zero in Jammu & Kashmir to as high as Rs. 2557/ha in Bihar.

Table 3.8

Average Area, Sum Insured, Premium Paid and Indemnities Claimed under NAIS by States

States	*Area/ Farmer (ha)*	*Sum Insured per (Rs.)*		*Premium Paid per (Rs.)*		*Claim per (Rs.)*	
		Farmer	*Hectare*	*Farmer*	*Hectare*	*Farmer*	*Hectare*
Andhra Pradesh	1.52	13211	8675	365	239	965	634
Assam	0.75	8234	10979	207	276	179	239
Bihar	1.12	11469	10207	250	222	2873	2557
Chhattisgarh	2.18	5636	2582	146	67	488	224
Goa	1.60	4017	2511	71	44	45	28
Gujarat	2.44	17614	7209	781	320	2938	1202
Haryana	1.25	8187	6536	258	206	69	55
Himachal Pradesh	0.61	4840	7883	111	181	466	760
Jammu & Kashmir	1.38	6770	4923	128	93	0	0
Jharkhand	0.56	3886	6954	94	169	1195	2139
Karnataka	1.62	10526	6511	342	212	1691	1046
Kerala	0.85	11195	13246	234	277	629	744
Madhya Pradesh	2.70	7905	2925	241	89	429	159
Maharashtra	1.05	5898	5593	214	203	499	474
Meghalaya	1.09	8853	8115	560	513	262	240
Orissa	1.02	8767	8563	221	216	625	610
Rajasthan	2.43	10293	4244	286	118	829	342
Sikkim	1.00	11778	11778	119	119	128	128
Tamil Nadu	1.71	16110	9394	333	194	2135	1245
Tripura	0.57	9642	16874	278	486	184	322
Uttar Pradesh	1.49	9155	6152	180	121	300	201
Uttaranchal	1.06	9405	8897	147	139	108	102
West Bengal	0.52	6680	12763	174	332	266	508
Andaman & Nicobar	1.00	8852	8852	205	205	61	61
Pondicherry	1.56	19210	12295	378	242	902	577
Total (India)	1.63	9573	5860	295	180	915	560

Source: Authors' calculations based on data taken from AIC (2007).

3.3 Other Agricultural Insurance Schemes

Agriculture insurance in India till recently concentrated only on crop sector and confined to compensate yield loss. Recently, some other insurance schemes have also come into operation in the country which goes beyond yield loss and also cover the non-crop sector. These include farm income insurance scheme, rainfall insurance scheme, and livestock insurance scheme. All these schemes except rainfall insurance and various crop insurance schemes discussed above remained in the realm of public sector.

3.3.1 Farm Income Insurance

The farm income insurance scheme was started on a pilot basis during 2003-04 to provide income protection to the farmers by integrating the mechanism of insuring yield as well as market risks. In this scheme the farmer's income is ensured by providing minimum guaranteed income.

3.3.2 Livestock Insurance

Livestock insurance is provided by public sector insurance companies and the insurance cover is available for almost all livestock species. Normally, an animal is insured up to 100 per cent of the

Table 3.9

Progress of Livestock Insurance

Year	*Number of Animals Insured (millions)*	*% Livestock Population Insured*
1988-89	18.60	4.20
1992-93	13.80	2.90
1997-98	22.83	4.70
1998-99	23.50	4.84
1999-2000	17.10	3.52
2000-01	15.35	3.16
2001-02	16.49	3.40
2002-03	29.40	6.09
2004-05	32.18	6.58

Source: Various issues of *Basic Animal Husbandry Statistics*, GoI.

market value. The premium is 4 per cent of the sum insured for general public and 2.25 per cent for Integrated Rural Development Programme (IRDP) beneficiaries. The government subsidises premium for IRDP beneficiaries. Progress in livestock insurance, however, has been slow and poor (Table 3.9). In 2004-05 about 32.18 million heads were insured which comprised 6.58 per cent of livestock population. The implementation of the livestock insurance as it obtains now, does not satisfy the farmers much. The procedure for verification of claims and their settlement is a source of constant irritation and subject of many jokes. This calls for a re-look.

3.3.3 *Weather Based Crop Insurance/Rainfall Insurance*

During the year 2003-04 the private sector came out with some insurance products in agriculture based on weather parameters. The insurance losses due to vagaries of weather, i.e., excess or deficit rainfall, aberrations in sunshine, temperature and humidity, etc., could be covered on the basis of weather index. If the actual index of a specific weather event is less than the threshold, the claim becomes payable as a percentage of deviation of actual index. One such product, namely rainfall insurance was developed by ICICI Lombard General Insurance Company. This move was followed by IFFCO-Tokio General Insurance Company and by public sector Agricultural Insurance Company (AIC) of India Ltd. Under the scheme, coverage for deviation in the rainfall index is extended and compensations for economic losses due to less or more than normal rainfall are paid.

ICICI Lombard, World Bank and the Social Initiatives Group (SIG) of ICICI Bank collaborated in the design and pilot testing of India's first index-based weather insurance product in 2003-04. The pilot test covered 200 groundnut and castor farmers in the rain-fed district of Mahaboobnagar, Andhra Pradesh. The policy was linked to crop loans given to the farmers by BASIX Group, an NGO, and sold through its Krishna Bhima Samruddhi Area Bank. The weather insurance has also been experimented with 50 soya farmers in Madhya Pradesh through Pradan, an NGO, 600 acres of paddy crop in Aligarh through ICICI Bank's agri-business group along with the crop loans, and on oranges in Jhalawar district of Rajasthan.

Similarly, IFFCO-Tokio General Insurance (ITGI) also piloted rainfall insurance under the name—Baarish Bima—during 2004-05 in Andhra Pradesh, Karnataka, and Gujarat.

Agricultural Insurance Company of India Ltd., introduced rainfall insurance (Varsha Bima) during 2004 south-west monsoon period. Varsha Bima provided for five different options suiting varied requirements of farming community. These are: (1) seasonal rainfall insurance based on aggregate rainfall from June to September, (2) sowing failure insurance based on rainfall between 15th June and 15th August, (3) rainfall distribution insurance with the weight assigned to different weeks between June and September, (4) agronomic index constructed based on water requirement of crops at different pheno-phases, and (5) catastrophic option, covering extremely adverse deviations of 50 per cent and above in rainfall during the season. Varsha Bima was piloted in 20 rain gauge areas spread over Andhra Pradesh, Karnataka, Rajasthan, and Uttar Pradesh in 2004-05.

Based on the experience of the pilot project, the scheme was fine-tuned and implemented as "Varsha Bima-2005" in about 130 districts across Andhra Pradesh, Chhattisgarh, Gujarat, Karnataka, Mahrashtra, Madhya Pradesh, Orissa, Tamil Nadu, Uttarakhand, and Uttar Pradesh during *kharif* 2005. On an average, 2 or 3 blocks/*mandals/tehsils* were covered under each India Meteorological Department (IMD) rain gauge stations. The scheme covered the major crops provided at least two coverage options namely, seasonal rainfall insurance or rainfall distribution index and sowing failure insurance. Varsha Bima-2005 covered 1.25 lakh farmers with a premium income of Rs.3.17 crore against a sum insured of Rs.55.86 crore. Claims amounting to Rs.19.96 lakh were paid for the season. Further, during *kharif* 2006, the scheme was implemented as Varsha Bima-2006 in and around 150 districts/rain gauge station areas covering 16 states across the country.

The Weather Based Crop Insurance Scheme (WBCIS) of AIC was implemented in the selected areas of Karnataka on a pilot basis. WBCIS is a unique weather-based insurance product designed to provide insurance protection against losses in crop yield resulting from adverse weather incidences. It provides payout against adverse rainfall incidence (both deficit and excess) during *kharif* and adverse incidence in weather parameters like frost, heat, relative humidity, unseasonal rainfall etc., during *rabi*. It operates on the concept of area approach i.e., for the purpose of compensation, a reference unit area shall be linked to a reference weather station on the basis of which weather data and claims would be processed. This scheme is available to both loanees (compulsory) and non-loanees (voluntary). The NAIS is not available for the locations and crops selected for WBCIS pilot. It has the advantage to settle the claims with the shortest possible time. The AIC has implemented the pilot WBCIS in Karnataka during *kharif* 2007 season, covering eight rain-fed crops, insuring crops nearly 50,000 ha for a sum insured of Rs.50 crore. WBCIS is being implemented in 2007-08 on a larger scale in selected states of Bihar, Chhattisgarh, Haryana, Madhya Pradesh, Punjab, Rajasthan, and Uttar Pradesh for *rabi* 2007-08 season and will be continued even in 2008-2009 also as a pilot WBCIS (Union Budget 2008-09, GoI). In order to effectively use weather insurance as an important risk mitigation tool, the density of weather stations has to be increased while streamlining and automating the network. The government would need to support the product on the same lines as traditional crop insurance.

Together, these above mentioned companies have been able to sell weather insurance policies to about 5.39 lakh farmers across India from their inception in 2003-04 to date. Though, weather insurance coverage was limited, it holds lessons for future programmes. Important distinguishing features of weather insurance scheme and yield insurance scheme are presented in Table 3.10.

3.4 Comparative Picture of Various Agricultural Insurance Schemes

A brief account of all the crop insurance schemes launched in India till date is provided in Table 3.11.

Table 3.10

Comparison of Yield and Weather Insurance

Parameter	*Yield Insurance*	*Weather Insurance*
Scope of insurance cover	Covers yield shortfall	Covers anticipated shortfall in yield due to adverse weather parameters.
Scope of perils covered	All natural and non-preventable perils	Rainfall, minimum and maximum temperature, soil moisture, relative humidity, sunlight, day length etc.
Target group	All farmers growing insured crops	Farmers and others.
Crops	All crops for which past yield data is available	All crops for which correlation is established between yield and weather parameters.
Scheme approach	Homogeneous area approach(*Taluk*/block/ *mandal*)	Homogeneous area approach (Jurisdiction of rain gauge).
Scope for introduction of insurance	Can be introduced for all crops with yield data	Can be introduced successfully for crops with good sensitivity to weather parameters.
Premium rates	High	Relatively lower and flexible.
Sum insured	Loan amount/ 150 per cent of value of production	Flexible. Can range from input cost to value of production.
Control on adverse selection/moral hazard	Relatively less control	Almost complete control.
Time taken for settlement of claims	May range from 6-9 months from occurrence of loss	Within two weeks from close of indemnity period.
Administrative set-up	Relatively large	Relatively small.
Transaction cost	High	Moderate and affordable.
Transparency	Not transparent	Transparent and easily verifiable.

Table 3.11

Various Schemes Related to Crop Insurance in India and their Features

Insurance Scheme	*Period*	*Approach*	*Crops Covered*	*Farmers Covered (Lakh)*	*Amount (Rs. Crores)*		*Salient Features*
					Premium	*Claim*	
Crop Insurance Scheme	1972-1978	Individual	H-4 cotton, groundnut, wheat, potato	0.03	0.05	0.38	Voluntary, Implemented in 6 states.
Pilot Crop Insurance Scheme	1979-1985	Area	Cereals, millets, oilseeds, cotton, potato and chick pea	6.23	1.95	1.56	Confined to loanee farmers, voluntary, 50% subsidy on premium for small and marginal farmers.
Compre-hensive Crop Insurance Scheme	1985-1999	Area	Food grains and oil seeds	763	404	2303	Compulsory for loanee farmers.
Experi-mental Crop Insurance Scheme	1997-98	Area	Cereals, pulses and oilseeds	4.78	2.86	39.78	For covering non-loanee small and marginal farmers also in addition to loanee farmers.
National Agricultural Insurance Scheme	1999-Continuing	Area and individual	Food grains, oilseeds, annual commercial and horticultural crops	971	2944	9857	Available to all farmers. 10 per cent premium subsidy for small and marginal farmers.
Farm Income Insurance Scheme	2003-04	Area	Wheat and rice	2.22	15.68	1.5	Insurance against production and market risks. Compulsory for loanee farmers.
Weather/ Rainfall Insurance	2003-04-Continuing	Individual	Food grains, oilseeds annual commercial and horti-cultural crops.	5.39	N.A	N.A	Available to all farmers. Based on rainfall received at the IMD/block rain gauges.

4

Farmers' Perceptions about Agricultural Insurance

Field Level Results from Andhra Pradesh

Field survey was conducted in Vizianagaram and West Godavari districts of Andhra Pradesh to assess the perception of farmers about agriculture insurance. The sample covers farmers who are currently availing agriculture insurance (called beneficiary) and those who are not currently availing any agriculture insurance. The main aim of the field survey was to know the perception of beneficiaries and non-beneficiaries of NAIS.

The primary data was collected from 150 farmers in district Vizianagaram representing rain-fed typology and West Godavari district representing irrigated typologies. The field survey was conducted during October 2005. From each of these selected districts, one *mandal* each with highest area/farmers covered under NAIS were selected. From the selected *mandal* three villages having substantial coverage under NAIS were identified. From the identified villages a sample of 25 farmers from different size of holdings were randomly selected. Thus, sample size consists of 1 state, 2 districts, 2 *mandals*, 6 villages, and 150 respondents. Details of selected villages and distribution of sample farmers is shown in Figure 4.1.

Information was also collected from the farmers who adopted rainfall insurance of private sector. Whosoever adopted private Rainfall Insurance (RI) in the villages selected for the study of NAIS were interviewed to get information about their experience and views about RI.

Figure 4.1

Sample Selection

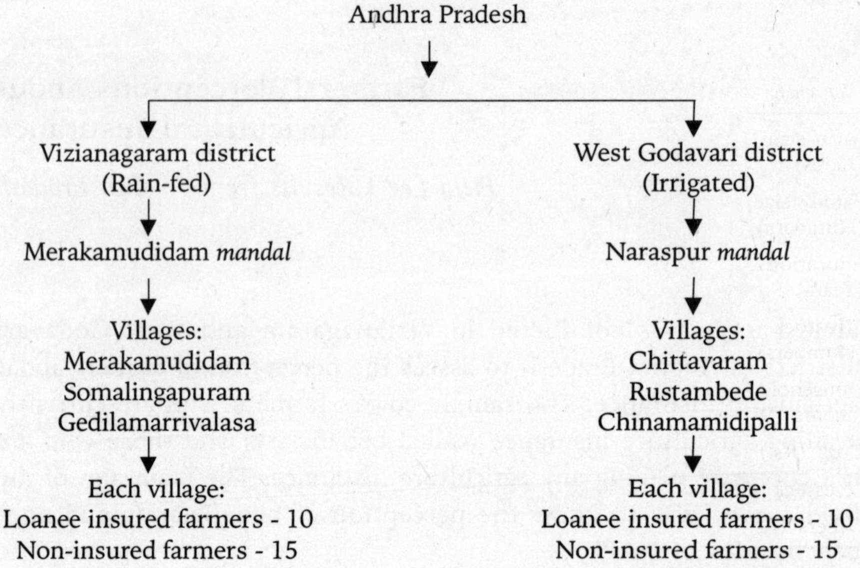

4.1 Socio-economic Characteristics of Sample Farmers

Socio-economic characteristics of insured and non-insured farmers are presented in Table 4.1. Average size of family among borrowers and non-borrowers was 5, and most of them have education up to middle level. Level of education, family size, and livestock ownership did not show any significant difference between borrowers and non-borrowers. However, farm size and crop income, which generally corresponds to farm size, were significantly higher for borrowers household as compared to non-borrowers. Income from other sources was higher at the non-borrower's households. Though the average income of the borrowers' household was much higher than the average household income of non-borrowers but the difference was not statistically significant up to 10 per cent level.

The borrower household took loan from a variety of institutional sources like cooperatives, regional rural banks, and commercial banks.

Table 4.1

Socio-economic Characteristics of Sample Households

	Borrowers n = 60		*Non-Borrowers n = 90*				
Parameter	*Mean*	*S.D.*	*Mean*	*S.D.*	*Mean difference*	*t*	*Significance*
Farm size (Acres)	4.82	3.42	3.47	2.35	1.35	2.87	***
Family size (Numbers)	4.90	1.53	4.99	1.13	-0.09	-0.41	NS
Education (Years)	7.78	4.12	7.66	3.62	0.12	0.19	NS
Livestock (Numbers)	1.54	3.02	1.68	2.66	-0.14	-0.30	NS
Household income (Rs.)	13396	36356	7800	19527	5596	1.22	NS
Crop (Rs.)	8916	23386	661	7644	8255	3.11	***
Livestock (Rs.)	1263	2826	1011	2949	252	0.52	NS
Others (Rs.)	3217	10150	6128	8934	-2911	-1.85	*

Note: *** Significant at 1 per cent level.
* Significant at 10 per cent level.
NS Not significant.

Amount of loan taken by a household varied in the range of Rs. 5,000 to Rs. 50,000 with an average at Rs. 19,665. Borrowers were asked the source from where they paid back the loan. Almost all the borrowers reported that they repaid the loan from the receipt from sale of agricultural produce. Only one sample borrower repaid the loan by taking another loan.

The borrowers were asked to what extent they would like the insurance agency to bear the crop loss, and to what extent they themselves would bear the loss. The response varies from 0 to 50 per cent implying that some farmers were not willing to bear any loss and want entire loss to be borne by the insurance agency whereas some farmers were willing to bear loss up to 50 per cent. On an average, sample farmers wants sharing of loss by insurance agency and farmer in the ratio of 82:18 per cent (Table 4.2).

Table 4.2

Loan Received and Risk Bearing Ability of Borrower Insured Farmers in Andhra Pradesh

Parameter	*Mean*	*S.D.*	*Max*	*Min.*
Average loan amount (Rs.)	19665	10729	50000	5000
Willingness to bear agricultural losses (%)	17.62	12.09	50.00	0.00

4.2 Response of Loanee Farmers

Views of sample farmers were solicited on various dimensions of insurance. These include motivation and experience with agricultural insurance, opinion on premium rate, and suggestions for improving the crop insurance scheme, etc.

More than three-fourth of the insurance beneficiaries mentioned that financial security was the motivation for going for insurance. Five per cent of the respondents considered bank compulsion as the reason for going for insurance. One respondent out of 60 described good experience of others as the motivation. Except two borrower beneficiaries all others expressed satisfaction with agriculture insurance mechanism (Table 4.3).

Table 4.3

Motivation and Experience of Borrowed Farmers with Insurance

Perception	*Response*	*Per cent*
Motivation for going for insurance	Due to banks compulsion	5.00
	Financial security	76.67
	Heard of good experience from others	1.67
	Above all combinations	16.67
Experience with agricultural insurance	Satisfactory	96.67
	Not satisfactory	3.33

More than 60 per cent of borrowers insured farmers felt that the existing premium rate was high while 32 per cent felt it was reasonable. Ninety-five per cent of the respondents would like to pay premium at the rate of 2 per cent while 5 per cent were willing for a range of 2-3 per cent (Table 4.4).

Table 4.4

Borrowers' Perception on Premium Rate

Perception	*Response*	*Per cent*
Paying premium rate	High	61.67
	Low	3.33
	Reasonable	31.67
	Can't say	3.33
Premium rate willing to pay	Up to 2 per cent	95.00
	2-3 per cent	5.00

Respondents made several suggestions for improving the existing scheme for crop insurance. A majority of the farmers want quick settlement of claims. Around one-fifth of the beneficiaries favour that crop cutting experiments used to serve as the basis for determining indemnity should be carried in the presence of affected farmers. Some respondents also propose reduction in premium rate and extension in insurance cover to more crops to improve the scheme.

Respondents were of the view that parameters to be considered for payment of insurance claims should be rainfall, crop condition and revenue reports.

Beneficiaries were asked to indicate their preference for the media through which awareness on insurance should be created. Village *mela* was the most preferred choice followed by television. More than 26 per cent of the beneficiaries indicate preference for more than one source (Table 4.5).

At present, service for insurance to loanee farmers is provided by the concerned institution like cooperative society or commercial bank. Close to 60 per cent borrower respondents suggested that rural agent at village level should facilitate insurance services. Some respondents want insurance service at their doorstep and some want it through cooperatives and post office.

Table 4.5

Suggestions Made by Loanee Farmers for Improving Insurance

Perception	*Response*	*Per cent*
Suggestions for improving insurance	Cover more crops	3.33
	Reduce premium rate	6.67
	Quick settlement of claims	56.67
	Gram panchayat as a unit of loss assessment	1.67
	Insurance service at doorstep	1.67
	CCE's in presence of villagers	21.67
	Above all combinations	8.33
Ad hoc payment of claims	Rainfall	13.33
	Crop condition report	31.67
	Revenue report	13.33
	All above combinations	41.67
Media prefer to know about insurance	*Kisan sabhas*	10.00
	Village *melas*	35.00
	Television	21.67
	Newspaper	1.67
	Film show in the village	3.33
	Road shows	1.67
	More than one opinion	26.67
Service provider for availing insurance	Rural agent at door step	13.33
	Rural agent at village level	58.33
	Cooperative bank	8.33
	Post office	3.33
	More than one opinion	16.67

4.3 Response of Non-borrowers and Not Insured Farmers

Those farmers in the same locality who were not currently covered by crop insurance were also interviewed to know their views on various aspects of agricultural insurance.

Majority of non-loanee farmers or farmers who were not availing crop insurance were aware about the scheme. Only 48 per cent of non-borrower respondents said that they were not aware about the scheme (Table 4.6). The source of awareness for those who know about the scheme was either bank or fellow farmers. About 82 per cent of non-borrowers mentioned that they never had availed insurance before while 18 per cent said they had earlier benefited from insurance. Several reasons were cited for not availing the insurance facility. Majority of farmers gave more than one reason for this. Lack of awareness about the scheme was the single most important reason for not availing insurance.

Table 4.6

Non-borrowers and Not Insured Farmers' Perception on Agricultural Insurance in Andhra Pradesh

Perception	*Response*	*Per cent*
Awareness of insurance	Don't know	47.78
	Banks	30.00
	Fellow farmers	22.22
Having insurance any time	No	82.22
	Yes	17.78
Reason for not availing the insurance	No awareness	22.22
	No need	2.22
	Lack of premium paying capacity	1.11
	Not aware of the facilities available	5.56
	Inadequate publicity	3.33
	Complex documentation	2.22
	Lack of cooperation from the bank	1.11
	Difficulties in opening bank account	3.33
	Non-institutional source of loan	7.78
	More than one opinion	51.11

These respondents were further asked what source they would tap if they suffer loss due to crop failure or other reason. Over 50 per cent respondents mentioned that they will go for hypothecation of house or jewellery or any other asset. About one-fifth of the respondents said they will take records to borrowing from moneylenders and 18 per cent look for borrowing from friends and relatives. Sale of fixed assets and bank loan were mentioned by a few respondents (Table 4.7).

Table 4.7

Non-borrowers and Not Insured Farmers' Perception on Strategy to Face Loss in Andhra Pradesh

Perception	*Response*	*Per cent*
Preference of agencies in case of losses	Sale of fixed assets	3.33
	Sale of livestock	1.11
	Borrowing from friends and relatives	17.78
	Bank loan	3.33
	Borrowing from moneylender	21.11
	Government relief	2.22
	Hypothecation of house/ jewellery/assets	51.11

The preference revealed by non-borrower respondents about insurance service is presented in Table 4.8. Like borrowed insured farmers, rural agents at village level were the most preferred agency preferred by for non-insured farmers. About 16 per cent respondents want rural agent at door step and about 28 per cent expressed choice for more than one agency.

Table 4.8

Non-borrowers and Not Insured Farmers' Perception on Preference for Insurance Agency in Andhra Pradesh

Perception	*Response*	*Per cent*
Service provider for availing insurance	Rural agent at door step	15.56
	Rural agent at village level	38.89
	Commercial bank	3.33
	Cooperative bank	5.56
	Self help groups	2.22
	Post office	6.67
	More than one opinion	27.78

5

Issues Related to Agricultural Insurance

Issues related to agriculture are of two types: one, issues concerning or related to existing scheme namely NAIS, and two, issues of general nature which go beyond the present mechanisms for agricultural insurance.

5.1 Issues Related to NAIS

The farming community at large does not seem to be satisfied with the partial expansion of scope and content of crop insurance scheme in the form of NAIS over CCIS. There are issues relating to its operation, governance, and financial sustainability. After extensive reviewing, gathering perceptions of the farming community, and discussion with experts from AIC, agricultural department, bankers, academicians, and other representatives in Andhra Pradesh on the performance of NAIS, some modifications have been suggested in its designing to make to it more effective and farmer-friendly.

5.1.1 Reduction of Insurance Unit to Village Panchayat Level

As of now, the NAIS is implemented on the basis of 'homogeneous area' approach, and the area (insurance unit) at present is the *mandal/ taluk*/block or equivalent unit, in most instances. These are large administrative units with considerable variations in yields and impact of natural calamities. For the scheme to become more popular, the unit for determining claim should be reduced to the level of 'village' in the case of large villages and to 'cluster of villages' in the case of small villages. However, because of infrastructural and financial constraints states could not lower the unit to village *panchayat*. Ideally, 'individual approach' would reflect crop losses on a realistic basis, and has been regarded most desirable (Dandekar, 1985). However, under the Indian conditions, implementing a crop insurance scheme at the "individual farm unit level" is beset with problems, such as:

- Non-availability of the past records of land surveys, ownerships, tenancy and yields at individual farm level,
- Small size of farm holdings,
- Remoteness of hamlets and inaccessibility of some farm-holdings,
- A large variety of crops, varied agro-climatic conditions and package of practices, and
- Inadequate infrastructure.

We feel that lowering of the insurance unit to the *gram panchayat* (GP) level, is a welcome move, as it would reflect yield losses at a reasonable level. However, data being the lifeline of insurance, the actuarial rating of the product at GP level would be possible only if the historical yield data at that level (GP) is available for a reasonably long period. In real terms, such data at the GP level is not available and therefore it would be difficult for the insurer to work out premium rates on sound actuarial principles (Planning Commission, 2007).

5.1.2 Threshold/Guaranteed Yield

Presently, guaranteed yield, based on which indemnities are calculated, is the moving average yield of the preceding three years for rice and wheat, and preceding five years for other crops, multiplied by the level of indemnity. The concept does not provide adequate protection to farmers, especially in areas with consecutive adverse seasonal conditions, pulling down the average yield. It is proposed to consider the best 5, out of the preceding 10-years' yield.

5.1.3 Levels of Indemnity

At present, the levels of indemnity are 60 per cent, 80 per cent and 90 per cent corresponding to high, medium and low risk areas. It is perceived that the 60 per cent indemnity level, does not adequately cover the risk, especially in the case of small/medium-intensity adversities, since losses get covered only if and when, the loss exceeds 40 per cent. Consequently, suggestion was made that instead of three levels of indemnity there should be only two levels of indemnity, *viz.*,

80 per cent and 90 per cent. But, these higher levels of indemnity may escalate the premium rates, and would increase the subsidy burden of the government. Therefore, it may be wise, to continue with the three levels, with upgradation of 60 per cent to 70 per cent. Since, the majority of crops are being covered presently in the 60 per cent level category, its upgradation to 70 per cent level would be a reasonable improvement.

5.1.4 Extending Risk Coverage to Prevented Sowing/ Planting, in Adverse Seasonal Conditions

The NAIS under the existing mode covers risk only from sowing to harvesting. Many a times sowing/planting is prevented due to adverse seasonal conditions and the farmer loses not only his initial investment, but also the opportunity value of the crop. A situation where the farmer is prevented from even sowing the field, is a case of extreme hardship and this risk must be covered. Pre-sowing risk, particularly prevented failed sowing/reseeding on account of adverse seasonal conditions, should be covered, wherein up to 25 per cent of the sum insured could be paid as compensation, covering the input-cost incurred till that stage.

5.1.5 Coverage of Post-Harvest Losses

In some states, crops like paddy are left in the field for drying after harvesting. Quite often, this 'cut and spread' crop gets damaged by cyclones, floods, etc., especially in the coastal areas. Since the existing scheme covers risk only up to the harvesting, these post-harvest risks are outside the purview of insurance cover. This issue was examined in the light of difficulties in assessing such losses at the individual level. One of the suggestions to address this could be to extend the insurance cover for two weeks after harvest.

5.1.6 On-account Settlement of Claims

The processing of claims in NAIS begins only after the harvesting of the crop. Further, claim payments have to wait for the results of crop cutting experiments (CCEs) and also for the release of requisite funds from the Central and state governments. Consequently, there is a gap of 8-10 months between the occurrence of loss and actual claim payment. To expedite the settlement of claims in the case of adverse seasonal conditions, and to ensure that at least part payment of the likely claims is paid to the farmer, before the end of the season, it is suggested to introducc 'on-account' settlement of claims, without waiting for the receipt of yield data, to the extent of 50 per cent of likely claims, subject to adjustment against the claims assessed on the yield basis.

5.1.7 Service to Non-Loanee Farmers

The awareness about the scheme is poor, partly due to lack of adequate localised interactions and substantially due to the lack of effective image building and awareness campaigns. For loanee farmers, with premia being deducted at the time of loan disbursement and claim settlements being credited to the farmer's loan account, the illiterate or poorly educated farmer is hardly aware of the scheme's existence, let alone its benefits. The poor participation of non-loanee farmers is even worse. Hence, major pilot studies, to build effective communication models, in this regard need to be conducted, as an integral aspect of policy planning.

NAIS being a multi-agency approach, the implementing agency presently has no presence, except in the state capitals. The scheme is marketed to non-loanee farmers through the rural credit agencies. These farmers are neither familiar nor comfortable in going to the distantly-located credit agencies. Dedicated rural agents, who could provide service, supported by the effective communication and training programmes, would be a needed initiative (Planning Commission, 2007).

5.1.8 Premium Sharing by Financial Institutions

Crop insurance claims are paid for adverse seasons, the loan availed of which in any case could not have been repaid by the farmer. The claim amount is automatically adjusted against the outstanding crop loan, leading to the recovery of dues for the financial institutions (FIs), and providing the farmer eligibility for fresh loan. In other words, crop insurance helps the flow of credit to crop production.

Considering the overall benefits of crop insurance and its direct and indirect protection to lending activities, the burden of high premium rates of crop insurance, may be partly shared by the FIs. Keeping in mind the collateral security provided by insurance, we recommend that 25 per cent of farmers' premium subject to a maximum of 1 percentage points be borne by the FIs, in respect of loanee farmers.

5.2 General Issues

Even several years after the initiation of the first agriculture insurance project in 1972, the coverage and scope of agriculture insurance remains far from adequate, even though the need for various forms of insurance for agriculture sector has been widely expressed. Some of the issues related to expansion of agriculture insurance and improving its effectiveness are discussed below:

5.2.1 Role of Government

As mentioned before, crop insurance, to be successful requires public support. This could be in terms of subsidy on premium, meeting part of administrative expenditure, and reinsurance etc. Global experience shows that due to special nature of agriculture production, in several countries, premiums payable by farmers is subsidised by government. Agriculture in India is not just dependent on weather conditions, but also suffers the brunt of natural disasters. It will be quite in order for crop insurance to be regarded as a support measure in which government plays an important role, because of the benefit it provides not merely to the insured farmers, but to the entire national economy due to the forward and backward linkages with the rest of the economy. Society can significantly gain from more efficient sharing of crop and natural disaster risks. The principle behind the evaluation of crop insurance schemes all over the world are along these lines for receiving the active support and finance of the government. Integrating the various risk mitigation methods and streamlining the funds not only injects accountability and professionalism into the system, but also increases economic efficiency. The support mechanism of major countries is given in the Table 5.1.

Government can facilitate agricultural insurance in several ways. In case farmers are asked to pay full premium themselves, then chances of adoption of insurance are bleak. There is a need for some subsidisation by government. It can provide information, on weather patterns, locations of farms and crops, incidence and history of perils, and crop yields. It can help to meet the costs of the research to be undertaken before starting an agricultural insurance programme. It can also provide reinsurance.

Table 5.1

Crop Insurance Support Mechanism of Major Countries

S. No	*Country*	*Nature of Support*
1.	USA (covered nearly 2 million out of total 8 million farmers and about 78 per cent of cropped area during 2003)	– Subsidy in premium (ranges from 38 per cent to 67 per cent; average for 2003 is 60 per cent) – Reimbursement of administrative expenses of insurance companies (these were about 22 per cent of total cost of the programme during 2003-04) – Reinsurance support for risky crop lines – Technical services in premium, policy guidelines – Free insurance of catastrophic cover for resource poor farmers – Non-insured assistance to farmers for crops, no insurance is available **Over all subsidy is about 70-75 per cent**
2.	Canada	– Subsidy in premiums (80-100 per cent for lower levels of coverage and 50-60 percent for higher levels of coverage) – Significant contribution towards provincial administrative costs – Provides deficit financing to provincial governments – Technical services by setting premium rates **Over all subsidy is about 70 per cent**
3.	The Philippines	– Subsidy in premium (ranges from 50 per cent-60 per cent) – Banks share premium of loanee farmers (15-20 per cent of total premium cost) – Financial support to Philippines Crop Insurance Corporation (PCIC) in extreme adversities **Over all subsidy is about 70 per cent for loanee farmers and about 50 per cent for non-loanee farmers**
4.	Spain	– Subsidy in premium (average 58 per cent during 2003) – Reinsurance support (50 per cent of reinsurance cost is paid by the government) – Technical guidance **Over all subsidy between 50-60 per cent**

Source: Report of *working group* on Risk Management in Agriculture, XI Five Year Plan 2007-2012.

5.2.2 Perils to be Covered

Fundamental issue in the design of a crop insurance scheme is whether to cover all or certain specified risks. The former implies yield insurance. In other words, an insured farmer is eligible to get indemnity if the yield is below certain guaranteed level for any reason. As it is very difficult to identify losses arising out of uninsured events, it is more practical to ensure yield rather than "yield loss due to specific factors". A scheme based on named perils is feasible if the insured crops are affected by specific perils, causing damage, which are measurable. If a scheme envisages coverage of all risks, it is necessary to provide adequate safeguards to minimise the incidence of moral hazard (Jain, 2004).

5.2.3 Involvement of Public or Private Sector

The above discussed crop insurance schemes that have been developed in the public sector are often of multi-risk or all-risk type. Most of these schemes are linked to agricultural credit. Public sector insurance companies are helped by government in various forms like: a) bearing fully or partly the cost of administration; b) sharing a part of the indemnity, or paying a part of the premium with a view to ensuring that farmers can afford to buy insurance.

Private agricultural insurance has been in existence from 2003-04 in the form of rainfall/weather insurance in India. Private sector insurance is voluntary and it covers specific risks which are insurable. There is no direct government support to private sector players (Sinha, 2004). It is worthwhile to seek increased involvement of private sector in agriculture by extending similar support to them as available to public sector.

5.3 Individual/Area Approach and Coverage

Agriculture insurance in India has been based so far mostly on area approach because of several problems associated with determining indemnity for individual farmers (Dandekar, 1976). However, pressure is growing from the farming community for individual approach. Obviously, 'individual approach' would reflect crop losses on realistic basis and hence, most desirable, but, in Indian conditions, implementing a crop insurance scheme at 'individual farm unit level' is beset with serious problems like (i) non-availability of past records on production and performance of individual farm to assess risk, (ii) monitoring of large number of small units, (iii) moral hazard, and (iv) high transaction cost. Innovative mechanisms need to be developed to gradually shift from area approach to individual approach.

5.4 Assured Value, Loss Assessment and Premium

Sum insured is usually based on cost of production or the amount of crop loan. In most of the schemes, the sum insured is based on the cost of production. The reason is that it is easier to assess the cost of production. Such cost of production data is available from independent sources like statistics and research organisations. This serves the purpose of area approach. There is a need to encourage farmers to maintain production/cost records, at least by farmers where some family member is literate.

6

Global Picture of Agricultural Insurance

The agricultural insurance schemes both in developed and developing nations are highly dependent on the government support in various forms like subsidy on premium, reimbursement of administrative expenses of insurance companies, reinsurance support for risky crop lines, technical guidance, and financial support. Subsidy on insurance premium in the recent years was estimated to be 60 per cent in the USA, 70 per cent in Canada, 50-60 per cent in the Philippines, and 58 per cent in Spain. Over 100 countries in the world have some form of crop insurance. The USA, Canada, Mexico, and Spain dominate the world crop insurance market in terms of premium. The total annual agricultural insurance premiums, worldwide, in 2003 was US$ 7.1 billion which amounted to 0.6 per cent of estimated farm gate value of agricultural production. As against this, premium to farm gate value of output in India in the same year was 0.015. Geographically, these insurance premiums are concentrated in developed farming and forestry regions, i.e., in North America (69 per cent), Western Europe (21 per cent), Latin America (5 per cent), Asia (3 per cent), Australia and Africa 1 per cent each (Roberts, 2005). It would be useful to draw lessons from the experience of other countries in agriculture insurance.

6.1 Lessons from Other Countries

In 1929, a group of farmers started a pool scheme which was the beginning of crop insurance in South Africa. Many hazards were covered in this programme, and hail was the main risk. Initially, multi-peril insurance was subsidised, but for the past 15 years it has not been subsidised. Many private players have now entered the field of crop insurance. These companies fix the premium amount based on the history of the particular risk. Estimation of damage is the biggest challenge faced by the crop insurers. Several crops such as maize, wheat, sunflower, and citrus are covered. South Africa is an example of how farmers can get the benefit of crop insurance through private companies even after withdrawal of subsidies.

As in India, crop insurance in Canada was implemented through an area approach. Research by Turvey and Islam pointed out that the area approach was not only unbalanced but also ineffective. The empirical research from different farms confirmed the belief that individual approach to crop insurance is better for reducing risk, but it also implies the use of higher premiums. The area approach in Canada proved to be inequitable, as it did not ensure a fair distribution of benefits among the farmers. Farmers with yields closest to the average would be the ones to get the most benefits.

In the Philippines, crop insurance programme is implemented through Philippines Crop Insurance Corporation (PCIC) which was established in 1978. Major crops covered are rice and corn. High value crops *viz.*, tomato, potato, garlic, and other root crops are also covered under interim insurance coverage. The coverage is limited to cost of inputs plus an additional amount up to 20 per cent, thereof on an optional basis. Multi risks cover providing comprehensive coverage. Coverage is available under: (a) multi risk cover, which is a comprehensive coverage against crop losses caused by natural disasters as well as pests and diseases and (b) natural disasters cover, which is limited to coverage against crop losses caused by natural disasters only. Premium rates are charged on actuarial basis. The government subsidy in premium goes up to 50 per cent. In case of borrowing farmers, lending institutions will also share part of the premium.

In Japan, the agricultural insurance scheme was established in 1947. At present, the scheme is composed of six programmes: rice, wheat and barley insurance, sericulture insurance, livestock insurance, fruit and fruit tree insurance, field crop insurance and green house insurance. The main features of the scheme are as follows:

1. The Central government reinsures the programmes.
2. In principle, implementation of three programmes, *viz.*, rice, wheat and barley insurance, livestock insurance, is compulsory.

3. As for rice, wheat and barley insurance, sericulture insurance, the participation of farmers who grow these crops over a certain size of cultivated area or a certain scale of operation is compulsory.
4. The Central government subsidises farmers with part of their premiums, and
5. The Central government subsidises the insurers with part of their office expenses.

In Sri Lanka the first experimental crop insurance scheme was established in 1958 as a pilot project covering rice cultivation only. The experience during the first 15 years period was quite favourable. The crop insurance board was established in 1973 under a parliamentary act to operate a comprehensive agricultural insurance scheme, covering all major crops and livestock. In case of rice and other crops, insurance protection was provided against lack of water, drought, excessive water, floods, diseases, insect infestation, damage by wild animals, and losses due to non-adherence to approved methods of farming. A large percentage (85%) of the total acreage insured is paddy and other crops that received agricultural credit. Due to increased cost of inputs, more farmers are expected to seek agricultural credit. A lending institution will not disburse any agricultural credit without proper insurance coverage. The coverage of insurance scheme is based on the cost of production. The scheme covers payment of indemnities of complete and partial losses as well as losses at various stages of production.

In the USA, the government supported crop insurance programme is implemented by about 15 private insurers, besides Federal Crop Insurance Corporation (FCIC), a government company. The programme is administered by the Risk Management Agency (RMA), on behalf of the US Department of Agriculture (USDA). Once a crop insurance programme is approved by the government, the RMA gets the premium rates calculated for different crops/states/counties by utilising the services of the National Crop Insurance Service (NCIS). Any approved insurer can sell these insurance products at the rates certified by the RMA. All insurers implementing the programme are eligible for the same level of premium subsidy, and the administrative and operating expenses of the insurer towards implementing crop insurance programme, are entirely reimbursed by the government. Since the insurance companies are implementing the crop insurance programme at a premium rate set by RMA, the government also provides a reasonable level of reinsurance support (Hazell *et al.*, 1986). The reinsurance support would be highest for developmental lines (new and unstable crops) and lowest for commercial lines (established and stable crops).

In Spain, the government subsidy in premium ranges from 20 per cent to 50 per cent, of which nearly 95 per cent comes from Central government and the balance from the autonomous regions. Crop insurance in Spain is a well developed product with systematic development of actuarial science and pricing, and standard loss assessment procedures. Insurance coverage is available for majority of the crops against most of the natural and non-preventable risks.

Spain has a unique model of crop insurance in terms of both the programme and the organisational set-up. Spain has, what is known as the Combined Agricultural Insurance System. The system started in 1980, has recently celebrated its silver jubilee. The basic feature of the system is that all insurable agricultural risks are covered by the private sector and all types of policies are subsidised by the state. Most policies are of the multiple risks type. The customers of the system are farmers who can take out agricultural insurance individually, or obtain coverage through cooperatives and professional organisations.

Participation in the system is voluntary. It is a system in which 'AGROSEGURO' operates, both in its own right and on behalf of the insurers, who make up the co-insurance pool. The system is based on an intricate partnership between the private and the public sector. The key players of the system besides farmers, are ENESA (Entidad Estatal de Seguros Agrarios), attached to the Ministry of Agriculture. AGROSEGURO (Agrupacion Espanola de Entidades Aseguradoras de los Seguros Agrarios Combinados), a pool of 40 private insurance companies which participate in a system of co-insurance; CCS (Consorcio de Compensacion de Seguros), a public enterprise with its own resources, operating re-insurer (under the control of the Ministry of Economy), etc.

A key feature of the Spanish system is the participatory approach. All stakeholders are represented in ENESA, which enables taking strategic decisions and fixing the framework for the system (annual plans) in line with their needs. For any given year, ENESA takes the lead in publishing the annual plan. On the basis of the framework set out in the plan, AGROSEGURO fixes the detailed conditions for all insurance products, in particular the regionally differentiated premium rates which vary according to risk exposure and also include administrative and reinsurance costs. Subsidies from the State and the autonomous regions are paid out by ENESA and channeled through AGROSEGURO to the insurance companies.

Based on experience from 1980 to 2005, of the total agricultural insurance income of 6.79 billion US$, the contribution of farmers towards premium was 3.08 billion US$ (45 per cent), and that of ENESA and the autonomous regions was 3.71 billion US$ (55 per cent).

Financial performance of crop insurance programmes in seven countries reported by Hazell (1992) is presented in Table 6.1.

Table 6.1

Financial Performance of Crop Insurance Programmes in Seven Countries

Country	*Period*	*I/P*	*A/P*	*(A+I)/P*
Brazil	1975-1981	4.29	0.28	4.57
Costa Rica	1970-1989	2.26	0.54	2.80
India	1985-1989	5.11	-	-
Japan	1985-1989	0.99	3.57	4.56
Mexico	1980-1989	3.18	0.47	3.65
The Philippines	1981-1989	3.94	1.80	5.74
USA	1980-1989	1.87	0.55	2.42

Source: Hazell, 1992.

Hazell quantifies the conditions for sustainable insurance as follows:

$$(A+I)/P < 1$$

Where, A = Average administrative costs,

I = Average indemnities paid, and

P = Average premiums paid.

As per Table 6.1, the ratio of indemnities paid to premiums collected (I/P) is less than one (0.99) only in case of Japan while the USA (1.87) stands next to Japan in controlling the loss followed by Costa Rica (2.26) and the I/P ratio is comparatively high (5.11) in case of India. However, the ratio of administrative costs to premiums collected is very high (3.57) in Japan when compared to the USA (0.55) and Costa Rica (0.54). The high administrative costs of Japanese crop insurance scheme were attributed to its robust organisational structure starting from 'farmers associations' at grassroot level up to 'National Agricultural Insurance Association' at the apex level. The operational dynamism of these associations largely contributed to the success of Japanese crop insurance programme, particularly, the indemnities paid. When it comes to the overall loss ratio, (A+I)/P, none of the above nations derived any advantage indicating that crop insurance programme whether for an advanced or a developing country, cannot be designed without sacrificing some of the preceding rigid requirements.

6.2 World Trade Organization Regulations

WTO allows subsidisation of premium in agricultural insurance. This step is one among the 'Green Box' of measures by which a government can support its farmer-producers. While this is a recent development, there has been an increase in demand by the commercial insurance industry for information from governments on agricultural insurance. These enquiries indicate that the commercial players are aware of these guidelines of the WTO and are encouraged to enter this area.

7

Conclusions and Policy Suggestions

Agricultural production in a country like India involves variety of risks. These risks arise from climatic variability, natural and man-made disasters, disease and pest outbreaks, accidental factors, and market uncertainties. Risk proneness in the absence of effective mechanism for protection against risk has several adverse implications for stability of agriculture production, farm income, livelihood, investment in farming and application, and adoption of improved technology. This underscores the need for effective mechanisms for management of risk in agriculture. An in-depth study of these factors was essential for developing technological and policy interventions to minimise adverse impact of risk and reduce the cost of managing risk, both at farm and sectoral level.

7.1 Conclusions

Despite progress of irrigation and improvement in infrastructure and communication, agriculture production and farm income remain highly vulnerable to natural events and market uncertainties. The risk is much higher for farm income than production. State-wise results show that only in the states where irrigation is very reliable, it helped in reducing the risk. Those states where irrigation is not very dependable continue to face high risk. In some states farmers face the twin problems of very low productivity accompanied by high risk of production. Neither infrastructure nor technology helped in reducing production risk in some low productivity states. There is a strong need to devise and extend insurance products to agricultural production to safeguard against the impact of loss to production and income.

In a country where agriculture is at the mercy of the vagaries of the monsoon and other factors beyond the control of the farmer, the importance of agricultural insurance is not in doubt and needs no emphasis. Insurance provides people with a reasonable degree of security and assurance that they will be protected in the event of a calamity or failure of any sort. The modern insurance sector can play a major role here, and considerably strengthen the financial security of farmers. Agricultural insurance is a more efficient instrument and an effective institutionalised mechanism for dealing with the problem. It helps to streamline the relief efforts, and reduces the direct and indirect costs on the national economy.

In the absence of formal risk sharing mechanisms, farmers rely on traditional modes and methods to deal with production risk in agriculture. Many cropping strategies and farming practices have been adopted in the absence of crop insurance for stabilising crop revenue. These measures to reduce the risk in farming were not only costly but also relatively ineffective in reducing risk in farming and to adjust to drought and scarcity conditions.

Agricultural insurance is one method by which farmers can stabilise farm income and investment, and guard against disastrous effect of losses due to natural hazards. Agricultural insurance can also be designed to protect against risk of price crash or market risk. Besides income stabilisation, crop insurance also helps the farmers to initiate production activity after a bad agricultural year. It cushions the shock of crop losses by providing farmers with some amount of protection. It spreads the crop losses over space and time, and helps farmers make more investments in agriculture. However, one need to keep in mind that crop insurance should be part of overall risk management strategy. Insurance comes towards the end of risk management process. Insurance is redistribution of cost of losses of few among many, and cannot prevent economic loss. Crop insurance protects farmers' investment in crop production and thus, improves their risk bearing capacity. Crop insurance facilitates, adoption of improved technologies, encourages higher investment resulting in higher agricultural production.

Crop credit insurance also reduces the risk of becoming defaulter of institutional credit. The reimbursement of indemnities in the case of crop failure enables the farmer to repay his debts and thus, his credit line with the formal financial institutions is maintained intact. The farmers do not have to seek loans from private moneylenders. The farmer does not have to go for distress sale of his produce to repay private debts. Credit insurance ensures repayment of credit, which helps in maintaining the viability of formal credit institutions. The government is relieved from large expenditures incurred for writing-off agricultural loans, providing relief and distress loans etc., in the case of crop failure. A properly designed and implemented crop insurance programme will protect the numerous vulnerable small and marginal farmers from hardship, bring in stability in the farm incomes, and increase the farm production.

Access and availability of insurance changes the attitude of the farmer and induces him to take decisions which, otherwise, would not have been taken due to aversion to risk.

Many of the risks insured under public insurance programme are essentially uninsurable risks. Moreover, they occur frequently and hence are expensive to insure. The financial performance of most of the public crop insurance has been ruinous in both developed and developing countries.

Despite various schemes launched from time to time in the country, agriculture insurance has served very limited purpose. The coverage in terms of area, number of farmers and value of agricultural output is very small, payment of indemnity based on area approach misaffected farmers outside the compensated area, and most of the schemes are not viable. Expanding the coverage of crop insurance would therefore increase government costs considerably. Unless the programme is restructured carefully to improve its viability, the prospects of its future expansion to include and impact more farmers is remote. This requires renewed efforts by government in terms of designing appropriate mechanisms and providing financial support for agricultural insurance. Providing similar help to private sector insurers would help in increasing insurance coverage, and in improving viability of the insurance schemes over time.

With the improved integration of rural countryside and communication network, the unit area of insurance could be brought down to a village *panchayat* level. Insurance products for the rural areas should be simple in design and presentation so that they are easily understood. There is lot of interest in private sector to invest in general insurance business. This opportunity can be used to allot some target to various general insurance companies to cover agriculture. To begin with, this target could be equal to the share of agriculture in national income. Good governance is as important for various developmental programmes as for successful operation of an agriculture insurance scheme. Poor governance adversely affects development activities. With the improvement in governance, it is feasible to effectively operate and improve upon the performance of various programmes including agriculture insurance.

7.2 Policy Suggestions

Agricultural insurance market is on the threshold of a spectacular growth. The government underlined its priorities for agriculture in 2004 by setting a target of doubling agricultural credit in next three years. A large chunk of credit for agriculture would be supported by insurance collateral. Agricultural insurance in future though is likely to be largely demand driven, the efforts of the government to support and finance insurance products and/or facilitate congenial environment as meaningful risk management tool would further enhance the potential and credibility of agricultural insurance.

Crop insurance programme works as collateral security, therefore also benefit banks. When claims are paid, banks first adjust the claim against their outstanding dues, and balance if any is credited to the farmers. Therefore, the crop insurance scheme also benefits the banks. In the Philippines, banks are made to share a part of the premium burden. For rice where the premium is 10.81 per cent, the borrowing farmer pays only 2.91 per cent, while the government pays 5.90 per cent, and the lending institution, 2.00 per cent. A similar arrangement can be recommended for participating banks in India. Such arrangement would also bring non-loanee farmers into the fold of banking network, thus institutional lending of crop loans.

Remote sensing is the emerging technology with potential to offer plenty of supplementary, complimentary and value added functions for agricultural insurance. The present technology available shall not only provide the insurers with tools like crop health condition, area-sown confirmation, yield modeling which are very important, but also strengthen the position of insurers *vis-à-vis* reinsurance market.

Some of the possible applications of for agricultural insurance could be as follows:

1. Estimating actual acreage sown at insurance unit level to check the discrepancy of 'over-insurance' (area insured being more than area sown).
2. Monitoring crop health through the crop season, and investigation on ground for advance intimation of yield reduction.
3. To check adequacy and reliability of CCE data.
4. Developing satellite-based crop productivity models for cereals and other crops.

There is a need to promote private sector participation in agriculture insurance. First license for the private sector, was issued in October 2000. As of today, there are ten private sector insurers in the general insurance business: Reliance, Tata-AIG, Royal Sundaram, IFFCO-Tokio, Bajaj-Allianze, ICICI-Lombard, HDFC-Chubb, Cholamandalam, ECGC, and Star Health. The latter two, are limited to only a few lines of general insurance. The fact remains that these insurers have not yet undertaken agricultural insurance to a significant extent. Only two companies in the private sector have initiated crop insurance, albeit on a small scale. ICICI-Lombard was the first company to experiment with rainfall insurance in 2003. The concept is further extended to weather insurance since 2004. IFFCO-Tokio General Insurance (ITGI), the second company in private sector, started piloting rainfall insurance since 2004.

The Insurance Regulatory and Development Authority (IRDA) has stipulated that every new insurer undertaking general insurance business, has to underwrite business in the rural sector to the extent of at least 2 per cent of the gross premium during the first financial year, which is to be increased to 5 per cent during the third financial year of its operation. Crop insurance is included in the rural sector insurance for this purpose. The business targets stipulated in rural insurance apparently are very small. Those who do not meet even these small targets, are getting away by paying penalties of nominal amounts. If private insurers are to be spurred to enter the rural insurance market in a significant manner, the business targets have to be raised substantially by IRDA.

The experience of government supported and subsidised crop insurance, and the recent entry of private insurers, raise questions about the co-existence of government and private agriculture insurance. One view is that the private sector will be unable to compete with government insurance, given the subsidies and access to the administrative machinery for delivering insurance. An alternative view is that given only 15 per cent coverage by government insurance, the private sector can carve out a reasonable market for itself, based on improved efficiency, better design and superior services. Here one can even think of public-private partnership in providing agriculture insurance as against public-private competition. However, it is possible only when crop insurance can be run in a more professional manner with clear objectives. Providing Government help to private sector insurers would help in increasing insurance coverage and in improving viability of the insurance schemes over time. There should also be insurance provided by seed companies so that farmers who paid high prices for seeds such as GM crops did not suffer in case of crop failure.

In order to promote public–private participation in agriculture insurance, GoI should follow the USA model to work out premium rate through an exclusive technical agency, and offer the product to all insurers. Insurers can implement the product, enjoying the same level of support and subsidy. As a variation from the USA method, the government would not provide reinsurance support and reimbursement of administrative and operating expenses, as these costs would be loaded in the actuarial rates. The government can decide whether or not different insurers compete in the same area, or allocate specific crops and areas to a particular insurer (Planning Commission, 2007).

With increased commercialisation of agriculture, price fluctuations have become highly significant in affecting farmers' income.

Accordingly, market risk is now quite important in affecting farmers' income. We feel that implementation of market insurance to cover price risk is much easier than yield insurance. This can be done by requiring interested farmers to register their marketable surplus with insurance agency or market committee at the time of sowing of crop. The insurance agency should offer insurance cover to include price guarantee which could be minimum support price in some cases or market-based price from the past. Farmers should pay premium for this kind of price insurance and initially government should share some burden of the premium. During harvest if price in the notified market falls below the guaranteed price then insurance agency should pay indemnity. Modalities to be worked out for implementation of this kind of model.

7.3 Prospects of Agricultural Insurance

The farming community in India consists of about 121 million farmers of which only about 20 per cent avail crop loans from financial institutions and only three-fourth of those are insured. The remaining 80 per cent (96 million) are either self-financing or depend upon informal sources for their financial requirements. Most of the farmers are illiterate and do not understand the procedural and other requirements of formal financial institutions and therefore, shy away from them. Therefore, while the institutional loanees are insured compulsorily under the NAIS, few non-loanee farmers opt for insurance cover. Share of non-loanee farmers who constitute 80 per cent of farming households is only about 15 per cent in the total famers covered under insurance. This is quite indicative of the big gap between the segment of agriculture covered, and that which is not covered by insurance mechanism. This also signifies the tremendous potential of agriculture insurance in the country, which can mitigate the adverse impacts that various uncertainties would have on the individual farmers.

References

Agriculture Insurance Company of India Ltd. (2008). *www.aicofindia.org.* Accessed 2006 to 2008.

Ashan, Syed, M., A.A.G. Ali, and N.J. Kurian (1982). "Towards a Theory of Agricultural Crop Insurance", *American Journal of Agricultural Economics* 64(3): 520-529.

Atwood, J.A, M.J. Watts and A.E. Baquet (1996). "An Examination of the Effects of Price Supports and the Federal Crop Insurance upon the Economic Growth, Capital Structure and Financial Survival of Wheat Growers in the Northern High Plains", *American Journal of Agricultural Economics* 78(1): 212-24.

Babcock, B.A. and D.A. Hennessy (1996). "Input Demand under yield and Revenue Insurance", *American Journal of Agricultural Economics* 78(1): 212-24.

Bhende, M.J. (2002). *An Analysis of Crop Insurance Scheme in Karnataka*. Bangalore: Agricultural Development and Rural Transformation Unit, Institute for Social and Economic Change (ISEC).

———. (2005). "Agricultural Insurance in India: Problems and Prospects". Department of Economic Analysis and Research, National Bank for Agriculture and Rural Development *Occasional Paper* 44.

Binswanger, H.P. (1980). "Attitudes Towards Risk: Experimental Measurement in Rural India", *American Journal of Agricultural Economics* 62(3): 174-82.

Chand, Ramesh (2003). "Minimum Support Price in Agriculture: Changing Requirements", *Economic and Political Weekly* 38(29): 3027-28.

Chand, Ramesh and S.S. Raju (2007). "Risk in Indian Agriculture: A Case of Six Major Crops", *Agricultural Situation in India* 64(7): 283-90.

CSO (2007). *National Accounts Statistics*. New Delhi: Government of India.

Dandekar, V.M (1976). "Crop Insurance in India", *Economic and Political Weekly:* A-61-A-80.

———. (1985). "Crop Insurance in India A Review, 1976-77 to 1984-85", *Economic and Political Weekly* 20(25&26): A-46-A-59.

Department of Agriculture and Co-operation (2007). *Agricultural Statistics at a Glance*. New Delhi: Agricultural Statistics Division, Ministry of Agriculture, GoI.

Department of Animal Husbandry, Dairying and Fisheries (2006). *Basic Animal Husbandry Statistics*. New Delhi: Ministry of Agriculture, GoI.

Hazell, P. (1992). "The Appropriate Role of Agricultural Insurance in Developing Countries", *Journal of International Development* 4(6): 567-81.

Hazell, P., L.M. Bsssoco and G. Arcia (1986). "A Model Foe Evaluating Farmers' Demand for Insurance : Applications in Mexico and Panama", in P.B.R. Hazell, C. Pomareda. and A. Valdes (eds.), *Crop Insurance for Agricultural Development: Issues and Experience*. Baltimore and London: The Johns Hopkins University Press.

Horowitz, J.K and E. Lichtenberg (1993). "Insurance, Moral Hazard, and Chemical Use in Agriculture", *American Journal of Agricultural Economics* 75(4): 926-35.

Jain, R.C.A. (2004). "Challenges in Implementing Agriculture Insurance and Re-insurance in Developing Countries", *The Journal:* 14-23, January-June.

Jodha, N.S. (1981). "Role of Credit in Farmers' Adjustment Against Risk in Arid and Semi-Arid Tropical Areas of India". *Economic and Political Weekly:* XVI(22&23).

Ministry of Finance (2007). *Economic Survey (2007-08)*. New Delhi: Government of India.

Mishra, P.K. (1994). "Crop Insurance and Crop Credit: Impact of the Comprehensive Crop Insurance Scheme on Cooperative Credit in Gujarat", *Journal of International Development* 6(5): 529-68.

———. (1996). *Agricultural Risk, Insurance and Income*. Arabury, Vermont: Ashgate Publishing Company.

Planning Commission (2007). *Report of Working Group on "Risk Management of Agriculture" for the XI Five Year Plan.*

Pomareda, Carlos (1986). "An Evaluation of the Impact of Credit Insurance on Bank Performance in Panama", in Peter Hazell, Carlos Pomareda and Alberto Valdes (eds.), *Crop Insurance for Agricultural Development: Issues and Experience*. Batimore and London: The Johns Hopkins University Press.

Raju, S.S. and Ramesh Chand. (2007). "Progress and Problems in Agricultural Insurance in India", *Economic and Political Weekly:* 1905-08.

———. (2008). "A Study on the Performance of National Agricultural Insurance Scheme and Suggestions to Make it More Effective", *Agricultural Economics Research Review* 21(1): 11-19.

———. (2008). "Agricultural Insurance in India: Problems and Prospects", National Centre for Agricultural Economics and Policy Research (NCAP), *Working Paper* no.8.

Rao, C.H.H., S.K. Ray and K. Subbarao.(1988). *Unstable Agriculture and Droughts-Implications for Policy*. New Delhi: Vikas Publishing House Pvt. Ltd.

Ray, P.K. (1971). *Review of Paddy Crop Insurance in Ceylon*. Colombo: Government of Ceylon.

Ray, S.K. (1983). "An Empirical Investigation of the Nature and Causes for Growth and Instability in Indian Agriculture: 1950-1980", *Indian Journal of Agricultural Economics* 38(4): 459-74.

Roberts, Raj (2005). "Insurance of Crops in Developing Countries", *FAO Agricultural Service Bulletin* 159.

Sharma, H.R. Kamlesh Singh and Shanta Kumari (2006). "Extent and Source of Instability in Foodgrains Production in India", *Indian Journal of Agricultural Economics* 61(4): 648-66.

Sinha, Sidharth (2004). "Agriculture Insurance in India Scope for Participation of Private Insurers", *Economic and Political Weekly:* 2605-12.

Smith, V.H. and B.K. Goodwin (1996). "Crop Insurance, Moral Hazard, and Agricultural Chemical Use", *American Journal of Agricultural Economics* 28(2): 428-438.

Tripathi, S.L. (1987). *Crop Insurance in India with Special Reference to Comprehensive Crop Insurance Scheme*. A note prepared for induction training programme in crop insurance for newly recruited assistant administrative officers of General Insurance Corporation of India, 9-28 November. Pune: Vaikunth Mehata National Institute of Cooperative Management.

Walker, T.S. and N.S. Jodha (1986). "How Small Farm Households Adapt to Risk", in Peter Hazell, Carlos Pomareda and Alberto Valdes (eds.), *Crop Insurance for Agricultural Development*. Baltimore and London: The Johns Hopkins University Press.

Glossary of Agricultural Insurance Terms

Actuarial

Describes the calculations made by an actuary. Essentially this is a branch of statistics, dealing with the probabilities of an event occurring. Actuarial calculations, if they are to be at all accurate, require basic data over a sufficient time period to permit likelihood of future events to be predicted with a degree of certainty.

Adverse Selection

The tendency of individuals with poorer-than–average risks to buy and maintain insurance. Adverse selection arises when insurers select only those coverages which are most likely to result in losses. In agricultural insurance, this can arise when:

- high-risk farmers or farmers using backward practices participate, while other farmers, with more certain production expectations, do not;
- farmers apply for insurance only on their own high-risk crops or plots, withholding other units.

Agricultural Insurance

Insurance applied to agricultural enterprises. Types of business include crop insurance, livestock insurance, aquacultural insurance and forestry, but normally excludes building and equipment insurance although these may be insured by the same insurer under a different policy.

Area Approach (area-yield basis)

An agriculturally homogeneous area that can be insured as one unit. This unit may comprise several blocks of land farmed by the same farmer or different farms farmed by different farmers. For loss adjustment in this approach, the actual average yield is assessed by simple survey through crop cutting or other methods, and compared with the normal (insured) yield. The average yield loss is applied to all land of all farmers within the defined area, disregarding individual differences in actual damage and crop yield.

Catastrophe

A severe, sudden and unexpected disaster which results in heavy losses.

Claim

The application for indemnity (payment) after an insured event has occurred.

Crop Credit Insurance

Coverage is decided based on the amount of the production loan of individual farmers. Each farmer has a different amount according to the different value of his loan, regardless of his cropped area.

Crop Insurance

Provides protection against loss or damage to growing crops including perennial crops such as tree crops against specified or multiple perils, e.g., hail, windstorm, fire, flood. Measurement of loss could be by yield basis, production costs basis, agreed value basis or rehabilitation costs basis. While most crop insurance is geared towards loss of physical production or yield, cover may also be provided to loss of the productive asset such as tree crops.

Drought

This is one of the most commonly requested perils by farmers, but it is also one of the most difficult perils to insure because of problems of its definition, isolation and measurement of effects on crop production. In contrast to most weather perils, drought is a progressive phenomenon, in terms of an accumulating soil moisture deficit for plant growth, and its impact on crop production and yields is often extremely difficult to predict, then measure and isolate from other non-insured causes.

Gross Premium

The premium paid by the insured, which is the aggregate of components including risk premium plus operating expenses, commissions, reserves and other expenses paid by the insured.

Guaranteed Yield

The expected physical yield of a crop stated in the insurance policy, against which actual yields will be compared when adjusting any losses.

Hail

Precipitation in the form of ice granules which according to the size and quantity thereof can cause severe damage to livestock and crops.

Hazard

A physical or moral feature that increases the potential for a loss arising from an insured peril or that may influence the degree of damage.

Indemnity

The amount payable by the insurer to the insured, either in the form of cash, repair, replacement or reinstatement in the event of an insured loss which amount is measured by the extent of the insured's pecuniary loss, is termed the indemnity. It is a set figure equal to but not more than the actual value of the subject matter insured just before the loss, subject to the adequacy of the sum insured. This means for many crops that an escalating indemnity is established, as the growing season progresses.

Insurer

The company which issues an insurance policy and is named in the policy as being responsible for paying a claim should a loss event result in damage to the insured property.

Livestock Insurance

This class of agricultural insurance generally centres on the provision of mortality cover for livestock due to named disease(s), and accidental injury. Insurance cover is normally restricted to adult animals and may be taken out on an individual animal or herd basis. Major classes of insured livestock include beef and dairy cattle, sheep, goats and pigs, and domestic fowl.

Loss Cost

Claims expressed as a percentage of the total sum insured or total liability.

Moral Hazard

The risk or danger to be looked for from human nature, both individual and collective. Moral hazard depends mainly on the character of the society, the character of the insured, and on the character of his employees and the manner in which they work and behave at work. Examples of poor moral hazards are carelessness, fraudulent claims, crime or arson, irresponsibility, gross over insurance, general moral climate due to period of depression and recession and unreasonable demand of high amount of claims settlement.

Net Premium

The premium necessary to cover any anticipated losses, before loading to cover commission and other expenses. Also called "risk premium"or "pure premium".

Peril

A potential cause of loss or damage to the property. Perils can be insured or uninsured, both are usually named on the insurance policy.

It is therefore important that loss adjustment procedures enable distinction to be made between damage caused by insured and uninsured perils. This main natural perils covered in agricultural insurance include fire, flood, freeze, hail, wind, excess rain, drought.

Premium

The monetary consideration payable by the insured to the insurers for the period (or term) of insurance granted by the policy.

Reinsurance

When the total exposure of a risk or group of risks presents a hazard beyond the limit which is prudent for an insurance company to carry, the insurance company may purchase reinsurance i.e., insurance of the insurance. Reinsurance has many advantages including: (i) leveling out the results of the insurance company over a period of time; (ii) limiting the exposure of individual risks and restricting losses paid out by the insurance company; (iii) may increase an insurance company's solvency margin (per cent of capital and reserves to net premium income), hence the company's financial strength; (iv) The reinsurer participates in the profits of the insurance company, but also contributes to the losses, the net result being a more stable loss ratio over the period of insurance.

Risk

1) The subject matter of insurance; the insured property. 2) Uncertainty attached to the outcome of an event. 3) The probability of a loss. 4) The insured peril. 5) Danger.

Risk Management

Care of risk to maintain income and avoid/reduce loss or damage to a property resulting from undesirable events. Risk management therefore involves identifying, analysing and quantifying risks and taking appropriate measures to prevent or minimise losses. Risk management may involve physical treatment, such as spraying a crop against aphids or planting windbreaks and/or financial treatment, e.g., hedging, insurance, and self-insurance.

Sum Insured

The amount specified in the policy up to which the insurer will pay indemnities should the insured peril(s) occur and result in a loss to the insured property.

Uncertainty

Not knowing whether an event is going to occur and being unable to measure the likelihood of occurrence of the event.

Underwriter

An individual who accepts risks and states the terms under which he is prepared to insure the property.

Agricultural Insurance Companies and their Services

S.No	*Insurance Company*	*Services*
1.	Agriculture Insurance Company of India	National Agricultural Insurance Scheme for crops, Seed Crop Insurance, Varsha Bhima, Weather Based Crop Insurance Scheme.
2.	National Insurance Co.Ltd	Rural Insurance—Cattle, Sheep, Goat, Poultry, Prawn, Silkworm, Horticulture, Plantation, Pump sets etc.
3.	United India Insurance Co.Ltd	Cattle, Poultry, Agricultural pump set, *Gramin* accident, Plantation, animal driven cart, *Tonga.*
4.	New India Assurance Co.Ltd.	Rural Insurance—Cattle, Sheep, Goat, Poultry, Prawn, Silkworm, Horticulture, Plantation, Pump sets etc.
5.	Oriental Insurance Co.Ltd.	Agriculture, Sericulture, Poultry etc.
6.	ICICI Lombard General Insurance Company Ltd.	Rainfall Insurance
7.	IFFCO-Tokio General Insurance Company Ltd.	Barish Bima

Index

Y